Renewals
01159 293388

 www.bromley.gov.uk/libraries

THE LONDON BOROUGH
www.bromley.gov.uk

Please return/renew this item
by the last date shown.
Books may also be renewed by
phone and Internet.

D1332793

HEINLE
CENGAGE Learning

Australia • Bra... ...m • United States

HEINLE
CENGAGE Learning

Frankenstein: The ELT Graphic Novel
Mary Shelley
Script by Jason Cobley
Adapted for ELT by Brigit Viney

Publisher: Jason Mann

Editor in Chief: Clive Bryant

Development Editor: Jennifer Nunan

Contributing Writer: Amanda Cole

Marketing Manager: Marcin Wojtynski

Content Project Editor: Natalie Griffith

Manufacturing Manager: Helen Mason

Art Director: Jon Haward

Linework: Declan Shalvey

Colouring: Jason Cardy and Kat Nicholson

Lettering: Terry Wiley

Cover / Text Designer: Jo Wheeler

Compositor: Jo Wheeler, Jenny Placentino and Macmillan Publishing Solutions

Audio: EFS Television Production Ltd.

For permission to use material from this text or product, submit all requests online at **cengage.com/permissions**

Further permissions questions can be emailed to **permissionrequest@cengage.com**

ISBN: 978-1-4240-3181-8

Heinle
High Holborn House, 50-51 Bedford Row
London WC1R 4LR

Cengage Learning is a leading provider of customized learning solutions with office locations around the globe, including Singapore, the United Kingdom, Australia, Mexico, Brazil and Japan. Locate our local office at: **international.cengage.com/region**

Cengage Learning products are represented in Canada by Nelson Education, Ltd.

Visit Heinle online at **elt.heinle.com**
Visit our corporate website at **cengage.com**

Published in association with Classical Comics Ltd.

Printed in Mexico
5 6 7 8 9 10 – 12

Contents

Characters

Victor Frankenstein

Frankenstein's Monster

Elizabeth Lavenza
Victor's adopted sister

Robert Walton
Adventurer

The Ship's Master

The Ship's Officer

Alphonse Frankenstein
Victor's father

Caroline Frankenstein
Victor's mother

Ernest Frankenstein
Victor's brother

William Frankenstein
Victor's brother

Henry Clerval
Victor's friend

Justine Moritz
Servant to Frankenstein's family

Characters

Monsieur Krempe
*Professor of Natural Science,
University of Ingolstadt*

Monsieur Waldman
*Professor of Chemistry,
University of Ingolstadt*

Lawyer
*States the charge against
Justine Moritz*

Old Woman
*Gives evidence against
Justine Mortiz*

Monsieur De Lacey
Cottager

Agatha De Lacey
*Cottager, daughter of
Monsieur De Lacey*

Felix De Lacey
*Cottager, son of
Monsieur De Lacey*

Turkish Merchant

Safie
Daughter of the Turkish Merchant

Mr Kirwin
Magistrate

Fisherman

Genevan Judge

Introduction

Mary Shelley's classic novel *Frankenstein* was first published in 1818. It was written in the days before steam travel when the world seemed much bigger than it does today. Only the bravest adventurers could visit distant places and discover the secrets they held. It was possible that things could exist — things even created by man himself — that would terrify anyone who saw them.

Science was progressing extremely quickly and it seemed that anything and everything was possible, as humans found new and powerful ways to create and to destroy.

At the same time, medicine was finding new ways to make the sick better and to make people live longer, which started to raise questions about the nature of life itself. For example, if a dying man could be saved and brought back to life, then could a dead man also be brought back to life? How about a dead person that was made from parts of other dead people? Could that be given life as well?

Where would it end? Would it go too far?

Indeed, in these early days of scientific advances, anything and everything seemed possible ...

NEAR THE COAST OF RUSSIA ...
FROM THE LETTERS OF ROBERT WALTON

LETTER 1 - DECEMBER 11TH, 17--

MY DEAR SISTER,
I AM ALREADY FAR FROM LONDON;
I CAN FEEL A COLD NORTHERN WIND
ON MY FACE WHICH FILLS ME WITH
HAPPINESS. IT GIVES ME A TASTE OF
THE WONDERFUL PLACE I AM GOING TO.
AT THE NORTH POLE, MARGARET, THE
SUN IS ALWAYS IN THE SKY. IT IS A LAND
OF BEAUTY AND AMAZING SIGHTS.

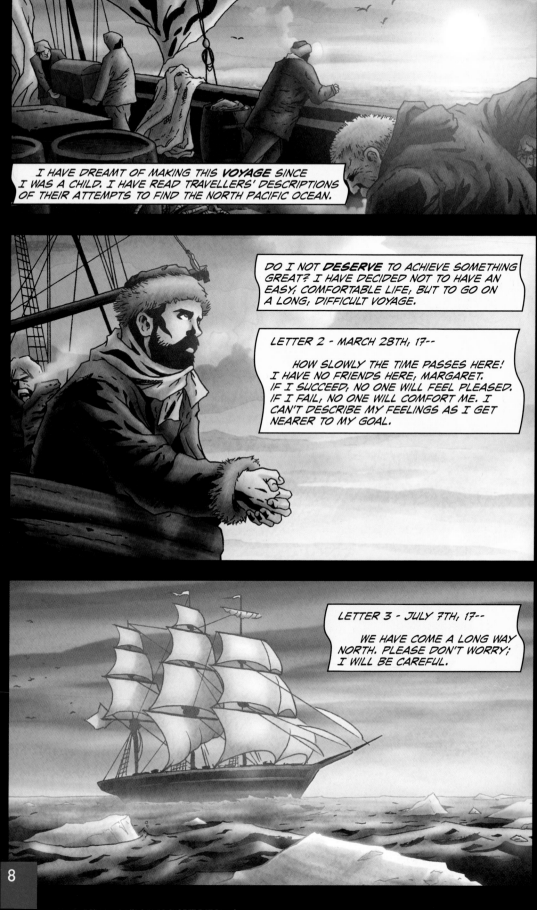

I HAVE DREAMT OF MAKING THIS **VOYAGE** SINCE I WAS A CHILD. I HAVE READ TRAVELLERS' DESCRIPTIONS OF THEIR ATTEMPTS TO FIND THE NORTH PACIFIC OCEAN.

DO I NOT **DESERVE** TO ACHIEVE SOMETHING GREAT? I HAVE DECIDED NOT TO HAVE AN EASY, COMFORTABLE LIFE, BUT TO GO ON A LONG, DIFFICULT VOYAGE.

LETTER 2 - MARCH 28TH, 17--

HOW SLOWLY THE TIME PASSES HERE! I HAVE NO FRIENDS HERE, MARGARET. IF I SUCCEED, NO ONE WILL FEEL PLEASED. IF I FAIL, NO ONE WILL COMFORT ME. I CAN'T DESCRIBE MY FEELINGS AS I GET NEARER TO MY GOAL.

LETTER 3 - JULY 7TH, 17--

WE HAVE COME A LONG WAY NORTH. PLEASE DON'T WORRY; I WILL BE CAREFUL.

LAST MONDAY, THE SHIP WAS NEARLY **SURROUNDED** BY ICE AND THERE WAS A VERY THICK FOG. WE DECIDED TO STOP MOVING AND TO WAIT FOR A CHANGE IN THE WEATHER.

AT TWO O'CLOCK, THE FOG DISAPPEARED AND THERE WAS ICE EVERYWHERE – AS FAR AS WE COULD SEE. WE WERE WORRIED; AND THEN, IN THE DISTANCE, WE SAW SOMETHING STRANGE.

IT WAS A **SLEDGE**, ABOUT HALF A MILE AWAY. A HUGE MAN WAS DRIVING IT. WE WERE AMAZED TO SEE SOMEONE SO FAR FROM LAND. WE WERE UNABLE TO FOLLOW HIM BECAUSE WE WERE STUCK IN THE ICE.

THE NEXT MORNING WHEN I WOKE UP, ALL THE SAILORS WERE TALKING TO SOMEONE IN THE SEA. IT WAS, IN FACT, A SIMILAR **SLEDGE**, WHICH HAD COME TOWARDS US IN THE NIGHT ON A LARGE PIECE OF ICE. THE MAN ABOARD WAS NOT HUGE, LIKE THE OTHER TRAVELLER, BUT A **EUROPEAN**. THE SAILORS WERE **PERSUADING** HIM TO COME ONTO THE SHIP:

HERE IS OUR **CAPTAIN**, AND HE WON'T LET YOU DIE OUT ON THE ICE.

COULD YOU TELL ME WHERE YOU'RE GOING?

WE'RE ON A **VOYAGE** OF DISCOVERY TO THE NORTH POLE.

WHEN HE HEARD THIS, HE AGREED TO COME ON **BOARD**.

HE WAS NEARLY **FROZEN** AND EXTREMELY THIN. I HAVE NEVER SEEN A MAN IN SUCH A TERRIBLE STATE. SLOWLY, WE HELPED HIM **RECOVER**. TWO DAYS PASSED BEFORE HE WAS ABLE TO SPEAK.

FOR SEVERAL YEARS I WAS THEIR ONLY CHILD. THEY LOVED ME DEEPLY.

WHEN I WAS ABOUT FIVE YEARS OLD, MY MOTHER **ADOPTED** A LITTLE GIRL. SHE WAS THE DAUGHTER OF A **NOBLEMAN** WHO HAD DIED.

ELIZABETH LAVENZA BECAME MORE THAN A SISTER TO ME. WE DID EVERYTHING TOGETHER. I LOVED HER VERY MUCH.

VOLUME I
CHAPTER II

WE WERE BROUGHT UP TOGETHER; THERE WAS LESS THAN A YEAR BETWEEN OUR AGES.

WHEN MY PARENTS HAD ANOTHER SON, WE WENT BACK TO GENEVA AND SETTLED THERE.

IN GENEVA, I BECAME CLOSE FRIENDS WITH HENRY CLERVAL. HE LOVED READING AND WRITING STORIES.

ELIZABETH WAS KIND AND LOVING, AND SHOWED CLERVAL THE BEAUTY OF GOODNESS.

I READ WITH **GREAT PLEASURE** THE WORKS OF MEN WHO HAD STUDIED NATURE AND DISCOVERED ITS SECRETS.

I BECAME THEIR FOLLOWER. I DIDN'T WANT MONEY, BUT I WANTED THE **GLORY** OF A GREAT DISCOVERY.

I WANTED TO FREE PEOPLE FROM **DISEASE**.

WHEN I WAS FIFTEEN, I **WITNESSED** A TERRIBLE STORM.

THE **THUNDER** WAS FRIGHTENINGLY LOUD.

CRACK!

AS I WATCHED THE STORM, A **STREAM** OF FIRE SUDDENLY CAME OUT OF AN OLD TREE NEAR OUR HOUSE.

WHEN THE FIRE DIED OUT, MOST OF THE TREE HAD DISAPPEARED.

THE NEXT MORNING WE FOUND THAT THE BOTTOM OF THE TREE WAS BROKEN INTO LONG THIN PIECES. I BECAME INTERESTED IN ELECTRICITY AND I BEGAN TO STUDY MATHEMATICS AND OTHER SCIENCES.

BUT **DESTINY** WAS TOO POWERFUL. SHE HAD ALREADY DECIDED ON MY DESTRUCTION.

VOLUME I
CHAPTER III

WHEN I WAS SEVENTEEN, MY PARENTS DECIDED TO SEND ME TO INGOLSTADT UNIVERSITY.

THEN ELIZABETH BECAME VERY ILL. MY MOTHER LOOKED AFTER HER AND SHE **RECOVERED**. HOWEVER, THEN MY MOTHER BECAME ILL.

My children, I always wanted you to marry each other.

Elizabeth, my love, you must be a mother to my younger children.

I'm sad that I have to leave you, but I will try to accept death cheerfully.

I hope to see you in another world.

SHE DIED CALMLY.

MY MOTHER WAS **DEAD** –

– BUT WE STILL HAD DUTIES TO PERFORM. ELIZABETH HID HER **SORROW** AND TRIED TO COMFORT US ALL.

FINALLY, THE DAY CAME WHEN I HAD TO GO TO INGOLSTADT.

WRITE OFTEN, VICTOR.

I LOVED MY BROTHERS, ELIZABETH AND CLERVAL, BUT I **LONGED** TO ACQUIRE KNOWLEDGE.

AFTER A LONG, TIRING JOURNEY I ARRIVED AT INGOLSTADT.

THE NEXT MORNING I DELIVERED MY LETTERS OF INTRODUCTION.

CHANCE LED ME FIRST TO ...

I FOUND A TRUE FRIEND IN **MONSIEUR** WALDMAN.

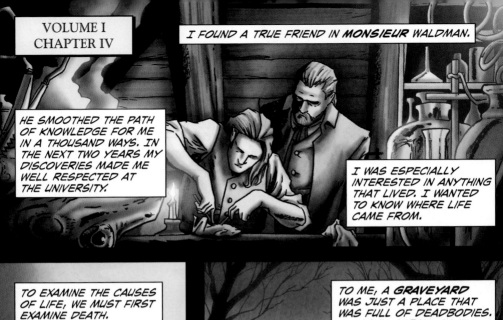

HE SMOOTHED THE PATH OF KNOWLEDGE FOR ME IN A THOUSAND WAYS. IN THE NEXT TWO YEARS MY DISCOVERIES MADE ME WELL RESPECTED AT THE UNIVERSITY.

I WAS ESPECIALLY INTERESTED IN ANYTHING THAT LIVED. I WANTED TO KNOW WHERE LIFE CAME FROM.

TO EXAMINE THE CAUSES OF LIFE, WE MUST FIRST EXAMINE DEATH.

I WANTED TO SEE WHAT HAPPENS TO THE BODY AFTER DEATH.

TO ME, A **GRAVEYARD** WAS JUST A PLACE THAT WAS FULL OF DEADBODIES. I WASN'T AFRAID OF IT.

FOR DAYS AND NIGHTS I EXAMINED DEAD BODIES AND HOW THEY **DECAYED**.

THEN SUDDENLY, AFTER WEEKS OF EXTREMELY HARD WORK ...

... I SUCCEEDED IN DISCOVERING THE CAUSE OF LIFE!

FOR A LONG TIME I WASN'T SURE HOW TO USE THIS **ASTONISHING** POWER.

I WAS ABLE TO CREATE LIFE ...

... BUT TO MAKE A BODY REMAINED EXTREMELY DIFFICULT.

THE SMALLNESS OF MANY PARTS OF THE BODY MADE MY WORK VERY SLOW SO I DECIDED TO MAKE THE BODY LARGER THAN NORMAL – ABOUT EIGHT FEET TALL.

MAKING THIS BODY WAS ALL I COULD THINK ABOUT.

ALONE IN MY ROOM, I WORKED ON MY CREATION.

OFTEN I HATED WHAT I WAS DOING.

I WORKED SO HARD THAT I BECAME ILL AND VERY NERVOUS. I COULDN'T SPEAK TO ANYONE.

ON A DARK EVENING IN NOVEMBER, I FINALLY FINISHED.

I PREPARED TO PUT LIFE INTO THE LIFELESS THING.

23

I SAW THE **MONSTER** THAT I HAD CREATED.

UNGHH... MUH...

PERHAPS HE SPOKE, BUT I DIDN'T HEAR.

ONE HAND REACHED OUT TO STOP ME, BUT I ESCAPED ...

... AND RAN INTO THE **COURTYARD**. I STAYED THERE ALL NIGHT. ALL THE TIME I WAS LISTENING FOR THE SOUND OF THE MONSTER.

HIS **UGLINESS** WAS INCREDIBLE. WHAT I HAD DREAMT OF HAD BECOME MY **HELL**.

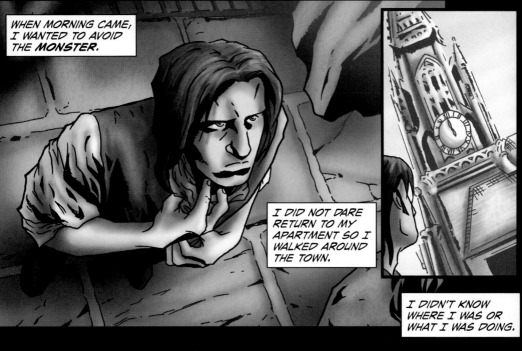

I WAS SHAKING NERVOUSLY AS WE WALKED TO MY COLLEGE.

I THOUGHT THE CREATURE COULD STILL BE IN MY APARTMENT.

I WAS AFRAID TO SEE HIM, BUT EVEN MORE AFRAID THAT HENRY WOULD SEE HIM.

HENRY, WAIT HERE FOR A FEW MINUTES.

I FELT COLD WITH FEAR ...

... BUT I SAW THAT MY ENEMY HAD GONE.

I CLAPPED MY HANDS FOR JOY AND RAN DOWN FOR HENRY.

THE **SERVANT** BROUGHT US BREAKFAST, BUT I WAS TOO EXCITED TO EAT.

HA-HA HA HA-HAH!!!

HA-HARRH!

VICTOR! WHAT'S THE MATTER?

HA HA HA HA HA!

WHAT'S MAKING YOU LIKE THIS?

I THOUGHT I SAW THE **MONSTER** IN MY ROOM.

HE CAN TELL YOU!

DEAR VICTOR,

YOU HAVE BEEN ILL, VERY ILL, AND I AM WORRIED ABOUT YOU.

GET WELL AND COME HOME. YOUR FATHER REALLY WANTS TO SEE YOU.

ERNEST IS SIXTEEN NOW. HE WANTS VERY MUCH TO GO ABROAD BUT WE CAN'T LET HIM LEAVE UNTIL YOU COME HOME.

AND LITTLE WILLIAM IS LOVELY. HE IS VERY TALL FOR HIS AGE AND SMILES AND LAUGHS A LOT. HE ALREADY HAS TWO LITTLE 'WIVES'! LOUISA IS HIS FAVOURITE. SHE'S FIVE.

DO YOU REMEMBER OUR **SERVANT** JUSTINE MORITZ? HER MOTHER TREATED HER BADLY AND SO SHE CAME TO US WHEN SHE WAS TWELVE.

YOU LIKED HER VERY MUCH. SHE COULD ALWAYS MAKE YOU FEEL HAPPY.

ONE BY ONE, HER BROTHERS AND SISTER DIED, AND HER MOTHER CALLED HER HOME. SOMETIMES HER MOTHER WAS SORRY FOR WHAT SHE HAD DONE. AT OTHER TIMES SHE SAID THAT JUSTINE HAD CAUSED THE DEATHS OF HER BROTHERS AND SISTER.
BUT NOW SHE IS AT PEACE: SHE DIED AT THE BEGINNING OF LAST WINTER.

JUSTINE HAS COME BACK TO US AND I LOVE HER DEARLY. SHE IS CLEVER AND GENTLE, AND VERY PRETTY.

I FEEL BETTER NOW BECAUSE I HAVE WRITTEN TO YOU, DEAR VICTOR. GOODBYE! AND PLEASE WRITE TO ME.

ELIZABETH LAVENZA

DEAR, DEAR ELIZABETH! I WILL WRITE IMMEDIATELY!

I WROTE, AND FELT VERY TIRED, BUT IT WAS THE START OF MY RECOVERY. TWO WEEKS LATER, I WAS WELL ENOUGH TO LEAVE MY ROOM.

I HATED NATURAL SCIENCE AND THE SIGHT OF MY SCIENTIFIC EQUIPMENT. I COULD NEVER TELL HENRY ABOUT WHAT I HAD DONE, OR WHAT HAD HAPPENED ON THAT TERRIBLE NIGHT.

HENRY CAME TO THE UNIVERSITY TO STUDY THE LANGUAGES OF THE EAST, AND I BEGAN TO STUDY THEM WITH HIM.

I FOUND COMFORT IN THE WRITINGS OF THE EASTERN *POETS*.

THEY WROTE ABOUT A WARM SUN AND GARDENS, AN *ENEMY* WHO BEHAVES WELL, AND THE FIRE THAT BURNS IN YOUR OWN HEART.

37

SUMMER PASSED AND WINTER CAME. I WANTED TO GO BACK TO GENEVA BUT THERE WAS TOO MUCH SNOW. SPRING CAME AGAIN.

HENRY SUGGESTED THAT WE WENT WALKING AROUND INGOLSTADT BEFORE WE RETURNED TO GENEVA.

WHAT AN EXCELLENT FRIEND!

FOR TWO WEEKS WE WALKED IN THE COUNTRYSIDE. HENRY TAUGHT ME TO LOVE NATURE AGAIN, AND THE HAPPY FACES OF CHILDREN.

I FELT VERY HAPPY, AND HAD NO WORRIES AT ALL.

BLAC

WHEN I RETURNED TO INGOLSTADT, I FOUND THIS LETTER FROM MY FATHER.

MY DEAR VICTOR,

YOU HAVE PROBABLY WAITED FOR A LETTER SO THAT YOU CAN ARRANGE THE DATE OF YOUR RETURN. SO HOW CAN I TELL YOU OF WHAT HAS HAPPENED TO US?

WILLIAM IS DEAD! THAT SWEET CHILD, WHO WAS SO GENTLE! VICTOR – SOMEONE HAS MURDERED HIM!

LAST THURSDAY WE ALL WENT FOR A WALK IN PLAINPALAIS. IT WAS A BEAUTIFUL, WARM EVENING, AND WE WENT FARTHER THAN USUAL.

41

COME HOME, DEAREST VICTOR. ONLY YOU CAN COMFORT ELIZABETH. SHE CRIES ALL THE TIME AND **BLAMES** HERSELF FOR WILLIAM'S DEATH. WILL YOU RETURN AND COMFORT US ALL?

YOUR LOVING FATHER,

ALPHONSE FRANKENSTEIN.

MY DEAR FRANKENSTEIN, THIS IS TERRIBLE NEWS. WHAT ARE YOU GOING TO DO?

I'M GOING TO GENEVA IMMEDIATELY.

I SAID GOODBYE TO MY FRIEND. AS I GOT CLOSER TO HOME, I FELT TERRIBLY SAD AND AFRAID.

ALTHOUGH IT WAS DARK WHEN I GOT NEAR GENEVA, I WAS UNABLE TO REST.

I DECIDED TO VISIT THE PLACE WHERE POOR WILLIAM HAD DIED. I *CROSSED* THE LAKE BY BOAT TO ARRIVE AT PLAINPALAIS.

LIGHTNING PLAYED ON THE MOUNTAINS AND *THUNDER* CRASHED ABOVE ME.

CRACK-DOOM!

WILLIAM!

THIS IS THE SONG OF YOUR *FUNERAL!*

43

AS I SAID THESE WORDS, I SAW A FIGURE IN THE DARKNESS.

A *FLASH* OF *LIGHTNING* SHOWED ME WHO IT WAS ...

... THE *DEVIL* THAT I HAD CREATED.

WHAT WAS HE DOING THERE? COULD HE BE THE MURDERER OF MY BROTHER?

I BECAME SURE THAT HE WAS.

HE WAS THE MURDERER!

WHEN I SAW HIM AGAIN, HE WAS AMONG THE ROCKS NEAR THE TOP OF THE MOUNTAIN.

HE SOON REACHED THE TOP ...

... AND DISAPPEARED.

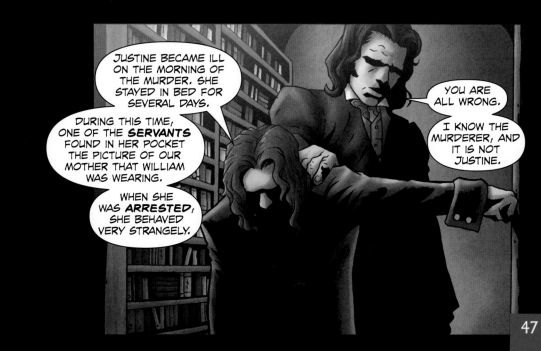

PAPA! VICTOR SAYS HE KNOWS THE MURDERER! HE SAYS JUSTINE IS *INNOCENT!*

IF SHE IS, I HOPE THE COURT DOES NOT DECIDE SHE IS *GUILTY.*

YOUR ARRIVAL, VICTOR, FILLS ME WITH HOPE. I SHALL NEVER BE HAPPY AGAIN IF JUSTINE DIES.

SHE IS *INNOCENT.* DON'T BE AFRAID.

VOLUME I
CHAPTER VIII

WE PASSED A FEW SAD HOURS UNTIL WE WENT TO THE *TRIAL.*

WHEN JUSTINE CAME INTO THE COURT, SHE LOOKED CALM AND CONFIDENT.

SHE LOOKED AT US LOVINGLY.

JUSTINE HAD BEEN OUT ON THE NIGHT OF THE MURDER. EARLY THE NEXT MORNING, A WOMAN WHO WORKS AT THE MARKET SAW HER NEAR THE PLACE WHERE WILLIAM'S BODY WAS FOUND.

I ASKED HER WHAT SHE WAS DOING, SHE GAVE ME A CONFUSED ANSWER.

JUSTINE WAS CALLED TO DEFEND HERSELF. AT TIMES SHE ALMOST CRIED, BUT SHE SPOKE CLEARLY.

GOD KNOWS THAT I AM COMPLETELY **INNOCENT**.

I SPENT THE EVENING AT MY AUNT'S HOUSE.

ON MY WAY HOME, A MAN ASKED ME IF I HAD SEEN THE CHILD WHO WAS LOST.

I SPENT MANY HOURS LOOKING FOR HIM. WHEN I TRIED TO RETURN TO GENEVA, THE GATES WERE SHUT. I HAD TO SPEND THE NIGHT IN A **BARN**.

THIS IS THE PICTURE THAT THE **SERVANT** FOUND IN JUSTINE'S POCKET.

ELIZABETH HAD PLACED IT ROUND WILLIAM'S NECK BEFORE HE DISAPPEARED.

A SOUND OF **HORROR** AND ANGER FILLED THE COURT.

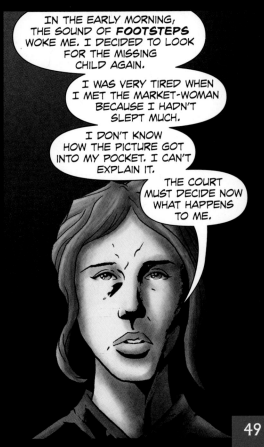

IN THE EARLY MORNING, THE SOUND OF **FOOTSTEPS** WOKE ME. I DECIDED TO LOOK FOR THE MISSING CHILD AGAIN.

I WAS VERY TIRED WHEN I MET THE MARKET-WOMAN BECAUSE I HADN'T SLEPT MUCH.

I DON'T KNOW HOW THE PICTURE GOT INTO MY POCKET. I CAN'T EXPLAIN IT.

THE COURT MUST DECIDE NOW WHAT HAPPENS TO ME.

ALTHOUGH ELIZABETH AND OTHERS SPOKE WELL OF JUSTINE, PEOPLE IN THE COURT WERE ANGRY WITH HER.

THE NEXT MORNING, I WENT TO THE COURT. THEY DECIDED JUSTINE WAS *GUILTY*.

... BUT SHE HAS **CONFESSED!**

HOW WILL I EVER BELIEVE AGAIN IN HUMAN GOODNESS?

I WILL SEE HER, ALTHOUGH SHE IS GUILTY, AND YOU MUST COME WITH ME, VICTOR.

OH, JUSTINE!

I THOUGHT YOU WERE **INNOCENT!**

I CONFESSED, BUT I LIED. I'M INNOCENT!

OH, JUSTINE! **FORGIVE** ME FOR NOT TRUSTING YOU.

DO NOT FEAR - I'LL **PROVE** YOU'RE INNOCENT.

YOU SHALL NOT DIE!

I'M NOT AFRAID TO DIE.

I CAN DIE IN PEACE NOW THAT YOU AND YOUR FAMILY KNOW I'M INNOCENT.

THE POOR SUFFERER TRIED TO COMFORT US ALL. BUT I, THE TRUE MURDERER, COULD NOT FEEL COMFORTED.

THE NEXT MORNING, JUSTINE DIED.

THOSE I LOVED CRIED OVER THE **GRAVES** OF WILLIAM AND JUSTINE – THE FIRST **VICTIMS** OF MY CREATION.

MY FATHER'S HEALTH WAS SHAKEN AND ELIZABETH WAS VERY SAD. I FELT DEEPLY TROUBLED. ONE DAY I SUDDENLY DECIDED TO LEAVE.

VOLUME II
CHAPTER I

I HAD WANTED TO HELP OTHER PEOPLE, BUT NOW ALL WAS RUINED. FULL OF **GUILT**, I NEEDED TO BE ALONE.

I HAD CAUSED SOME TERRIBLE **EVILS**, AND I WAS VERY AFRAID THAT THE **MONSTER** WOULD DO SOMETHING ELSE.

I WENT TO THE **ALPINE** VALLEYS BECAUSE I THOUGHT I COULD FORGET MY **SORROWS** THERE. AFTER A TIME, I ARRIVED AT THE VILLAGE OF CHAMONIX.

VOLUME II
CHAPTER II

I DECIDED TO CLIMB TO THE TOP OF MONTANVERT. I REMEMBERED THE VIEW FROM THE TOP. IT HAD HAD A GREAT EFFECT ON ME WHEN I FIRST SAW IT.

THE CLIMB WAS DANGEROUS. THE TOPS OF THE MOUNTAINS WERE HIDDEN IN CLOUD AND RAIN FELL HEAVILY FROM THE DARK SKY.

IT WAS NEARLY NOON WHEN I ARRIVED AT THE TOP OF THE MOUNTAIN. I SAT ON A ROCK AND LOOKED AT THE WONDERFUL VIEW.

MY HEART FILLED WITH JOY.

ALLOW ME THIS HAPPINESS, OR TAKE ME AWAY FROM THE JOYS OF LIFE!

AS I SAID THIS, I SUDDENLY SAW THE FIGURE OF A HUGE MAN. IT WAS COMING TOWARDS ME AT GREAT SPEED.

IT WAS THE **MONSTER** THAT I HAD CREATED. I SHOOK WITH ANGER AND **HORROR**. I WANTED TO FIGHT HIM AND TO KILL HIM!

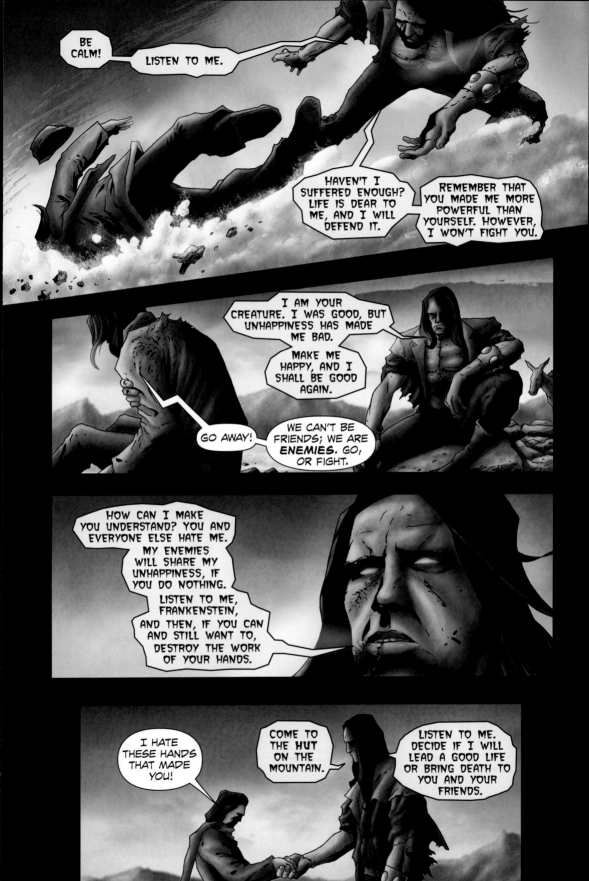

I DECIDED TO LISTEN TO HIS STORY. FOR THE FIRST TIME, I REALISED THAT AS HIS CREATOR, I HAD DUTIES TOWARDS HIM. I FELT I OUGHT TO MAKE HIM HAPPY.

VOLUME II
CHAPTER III

I CAN'T REMEMBER MY FIRST DAYS VERY WELL. I DIDN'T RECOGNISE MY DIFFERENT SENSES AT FIRST.

I WANTED TO FIND A PLACE THAT HAD **SHADE**, SO I WENT TO THE FOREST NEAR INGOLSTADT.

I ATE SOME FRUIT AND DRANK FROM THE **STREAM**. THEN I LAY DOWN AND WENT TO SLEEP.

IT WAS DARK WHEN I WOKE UP. I FELT COLD AND FRIGHTENED. I HAD TAKEN SOME CLOTHES FROM YOUR APARTMENT, BUT THEY WERE NOT WARM ENOUGH. I SAT AND CRIED.

SEVERAL DAYS AND NIGHTS PASSED. I SLOWLY BEGAN TO UNDERSTAND WHAT I SAW AND HEARD.

SOMETIMES I TRIED TO COPY THE SONGS OF THE BIRDS BUT I COULDN'T. THE NOISES I MADE FRIGHTENED ME INTO SILENCE AGAIN.

THERE WAS VERY LITTLE FOOD. OFTEN IT TOOK ME THE WHOLE DAY TO FIND A FEW NUTS.

I REALLY WANTED FOOD AND SHELTER. EVENTUALLY, I SAW A SMALL HUT. THIS WAS A NEW SIGHT TO ME. I EXAMINED IT WITH INTEREST.

THE DOOR WAS OPEN, SO I WENT IN. AN OLD MAN WAS PREPARING HIS BREAKFAST OVER A FIRE.

WHEN HE SAW ME, HE SCREAMED AND RAN AWAY.

I WAS SURPRISED, BUT I LIKED THE HUT VERY MUCH. SNOW AND RAIN COULD NOT GET IN THERE.

I HUNGRILY ATE THE OLD MAN'S BREAKFAST. THEN I LAY DOWN AND FELL ASLEEP.

IT WAS NOON WHEN I WOKE UP. THE SUN WAS WARM, SO I DECIDED TO TRAVEL FARTHER.

I WALKED FOR SEVERAL HOURS UNTIL I ARRIVED AT A VILLAGE.

AS I ENTERED ONE OF THE COTTAGES, THE CHILDREN INSIDE SCREAMED, AND ONE OF THE WOMEN FAINTED.

SOME OF THE PEOPLE IN THE VILLAGE RAN AWAY AND OTHERS ATTACKED ME WITH STONES. I RAN AWAY, BACK TO THE FIELDS.

I HID IN A SMALL **HUT**. THERE WAS NOTHING IN IT, BUT IT WAS NEXT TO A PLEASANT **COTTAGE**. I DIDN'T DARE TO ENTER THE COTTAGE AFTER WHAT HAD HAPPENED IN THE VILLAGE.

MY HUT WAS MADE OF WOOD AND WAS VERY LOW. I COULD ONLY SIT IN IT WITH DIFFICULTY. THERE WAS NO WOOD ON THE FLOOR AND THE WIND CAME IN, BUT IT WAS A GOOD **SHELTER**.

I LAY DOWN. I FELT HAPPY TO HAVE A SHELTER FROM THE COLD AND FROM THE UNKINDNESS OF HUMANS.

THE NEXT MORNING I DRANK FROM THE **STREAM** AND ATE SOME BREAD I HAD STOLEN. I WATCHED THE PEOPLE IN THE **COTTAGE**: A GENTLE YOUNG GIRL, AN UNHAPPY YOUNG MAN AND AN OLD MAN.

THEY SHOWED SUCH KINDNESS AND LOVE FOR EACH OTHER THAT I BEGAN TO EXPERIENCE NEW FEELINGS.

THEY WERE A MIXTURE OF PAIN AND PLEASURE. I FOUND THEM DIFFICULT TO BEAR.

WHEN NIGHT CAME, THE PEOPLE IN THE COTTAGE MADE LIGHT WITH CANDLES. I WAS SURPRISED ...

... AND PLEASED. I COULD CONTINUE WATCHING THEM.

THE NEXT DAY PASSED IN THE SAME WAY. I SOON REALISED THAT THE OLD MAN WAS BLIND. THE YOUNG PEOPLE SHOWED HIM MUCH LOVE AND RESPECT.

I WANTED VERY MUCH TO JOIN THEM, BUT I DIDN'T DARE TO. I STAYED IN MY **HUT** AND TRIED TO UNDERSTAND THEM. THEY WEREN'T HAPPY, ALTHOUGH I COULDN'T SEE A REASON FOR THEIR UNHAPPINESS. I WAS VERY AFFECTED BY IT. WHY WERE SUCH GENTLE CREATURES UNHAPPY?

LATER I DISCOVERED ONE REASON: THEY WERE POOR.

THEY ATE ONLY VEGETABLES AND DRANK THE MILK OF ONE COW. THEY WERE USUALLY HUNGRY, ESPECIALLY THE YOUNG PEOPLE. OFTEN THEY GAVE THE OLD MAN FOOD WHEN THEY HAD NONE FOR THEMSELVES.

WHEN I REALISED THIS, I STOPPED STEALING THEIR FOOD. I ATE ONLY FRUIT AND **NUTS** FROM THE WOOD.

I FOUND ANOTHER WAY I COULD HELP THEM. AT NIGHT I OFTEN BROUGHT THEM WOOD FOR THEIR FIRE.

I SPENT THE WINTER IN THIS **HUT**.

I BEGAN TO LOVE THE PEOPLE IN THE **COTTAGE**. WHEN THEY WERE UNHAPPY, I FELT SAD. WHEN THEY WERE HAPPY, I WAS HAPPY TOO.

FELIX WAS ALWAYS THE SADDEST. HE SEEMED TO SUFFER DEEPLY

BUT HE WAS ABLE TO GIVE PLEASURE TO HIS SISTER. HE GAVE HER THE FIRST LITTLE WHITE FLOWER THAT CAME UP IN THE SNOW.

I ADMIRED THE BEAUTY OF THESE PEOPLE BUT WHEN I SAW MYSELF IN A POOL OF WATER I WAS TERRIFIED!

AT FIRST I COULDN'T BELIEVE THAT IT WAS ME. THEN I FELT SAD AND ASHAMED. I WAS A **MONSTER**.

EVERY DAY I DID THE SAME THING. I SLEPT DURING THE DAY, AND WENT INTO THE WOODS AT NIGHT.

I COLLECTED MY OWN FOOD AND WOOD FOR THE FAMILY. OFTEN I CLEARED THEIR PATH OF SNOW. THIS SURPRISED THEM VERY MUCH.

I THOUGHT THAT I COULD MAKE THEM HAPPY. AND I WANTED TO WIN THEIR LOVE. TO DO THIS, I TRIED HARD TO LEARN THEIR LANGUAGE.

VOLUME II
CHAPTER V

FELIX?

MY SWEET SAFIE!

SPRING ARRIVED, BUT FELIX WAS STILL VERY SAD. THEN A VISITOR CAME.

FELIX WAS EXTREMELY HAPPY. THE LADY DIDN'T SEEM TO UNDERSTAND HIM, BUT SMILED.

THE DAYS PASSED PEACEFULLY. JOY HAD TAKEN THE PLACE OF SADNESS. FELIX BEGAN TO TEACH SAFIE HIS LANGUAGE. I WATCHED THEM CLOSELY SO THAT I COULD LEARN IT TOO. SAFIE AND I IMPROVED QUICKLY. TWO MONTHS LATER, I COULD UNDERSTAND MOST OF THE WORDS THE FAMILY SAID.

I LISTENED TOO AS FELIX TAUGHT SAFIE HISTORY. I LEARNT ABOUT THE MANNERS, GOVERNMENTS AND RELIGIONS OF DIFFERENT COUNTRIES.

COULD PEOPLE BE SO GOOD, SO WONDERFUL, SO POWERFUL AND AT THE SAME TIME SO **DREADFUL**? WHEN I HEARD THE TERRIBLE THINGS PEOPLE HAD DONE, I TURNED AWAY IN **HORROR**.

I THOUGHT ABOUT MYSELF. WHAT WAS I? I KNEW NOTHING ABOUT MY CREATION OR MY CREATOR. I WAS EXTREMELY UGLY AND I WASN'T THE SAME AS MEN.

THIS FAMILY – WHO WERE THEY?

THE DE LACEYS, FROM PARIS.

THEY CAME FROM A GOOD FRENCH FAMILY. SAFIE'S FATHER HAD RUINED THEM.

HE WAS A TURKISH **MERCHANT** WHO HAD LIVED IN PARIS FOR MANY YEARS. THEN THE GOVERNMENT THREW HIM INTO **PRISON** AND **SENTENCED** HIM TO DEATH.

THERE WAS NO REASON FOR THIS. PEOPLE SAID THE GOVERNMENT DISLIKED HIS RELIGION AND HIS **WEALTH**.

FELIX WAS BY CHANCE AT THIS MAN'S **TRIAL**. HE PROMISED TO GET HIM OUT OF PRISON.

THE TURK OFFERED HIM MONEY, BUT HE REFUSED. THEN HE SAW SAFIE AND WANTED TO MARRY HER.

FELIX TOOK SAFIE AND HER FATHER OUT OF FRANCE. THE MERCHANT ENCOURAGED HIS HOPES FOR SAFIE, BUT SECRETLY HE DID NOT WANT HER TO MARRY A **CHRISTIAN**. HE PLANNED TO TAKE HIS DAUGHTER AWAY.

THE *MERCHANT'S* ESCAPE WAS SOON DISCOVERED, AND FELIX'S FATHER AND SISTER WERE THROWN INTO *PRISON.*

NEWS OF THIS REACHED FELIX WHO HURRIED BACK TO PARIS.

HE WAS THROWN INTO PRISON TOO, AND HE AND HIS FATHER AND SISTER STAYED THERE FOR FIVE MONTHS.

THEN ALL THEIR MONEY WAS TAKEN AWAY AND THEY WERE SENT OUT OF THE COUNTRY FOREVER.

THE MERCHANT HEARD THAT FELIX HAD NO MONEY. HE TOLD HIS DAUGHTER NOT TO THINK OF FELIX ANY MORE.

A FEW DAYS LATER, HE LEFT FOR CONSTANTINOPLE. SAFIE WAS NOW ALONE. SHE FOUND IN HER FATHER'S PAPERS THE NAME OF FELIX'S NEW HOME IN GERMANY. SHE DECIDED TO GO THERE.

VOLUME II
CHAPTER VII

THIS WAS THE STORY OF THE DEAR PEOPLE IN THE COTTAGE.

I LEARNT TO ADMIRE GOODNESS AND TO DISLIKE THE WRONG THINGS PEOPLE DO.

ONE NIGHT IN THE WOOD, I FOUND SOME BOOKS IN A LEATHER BAG. I QUICKLY BEGAN TO READ THEM.

MY CREATOR HAD LEFT ME, AND IN MY ANGER AND UNHAPPINESS, I CURSED HIM.

I DECIDED TO INTRODUCE MYSELF TO THE PEOPLE IN THE **COTTAGE** WHEN THE TIME WAS RIGHT. MONTHS PASSED. THEN ONE DAY, WHEN THE OLD MAN WAS ALONE, I KNOCKED ON THE DOOR OF THE COTTAGE ...

KNOCK KNOCK

WHO'S THERE? COME IN.

PARDON ME. I'M A TRAVELLER AND I NEED A LITTLE REST. COULD I SIT FOR A FEW MINUTES BY THE FIRE?

COME IN, BUT AS I'M BLIND, I CAN'T OFFER YOU ANY FOOD.

I HAVE FOOD. I ONLY NEED WARMTH AND REST.

NOW IS THE TIME! SAVE AND PROTECT ME!

YOU AND YOUR FAMILY ARE THE FRIENDS I'M LOOKING FOR!

GREAT GOD!

WHO ARE YOU?

I CANNOT DESCRIBE THEIR *HORROR* WHEN THEY SAW ME.

AGATHA *FAINTED* AND SAFIE RAN AWAY. FELIX TORE ME FROM HIS FATHER.

MY TRAVELS WERE LONG AND MY SUFFERINGS WERE GREAT. I USUALLY RESTED DURING THE DAY AND TRAVELLED AT NIGHT.

HOWEVER, ONE MORNING I FOUND THAT MY PATH WENT THROUGH A DEEP WOOD. I DECIDED TO CONTINUE WALKING AFTER SUNRISE. IT WAS A BEAUTIFUL SPRING DAY, AND I FELT HAPPY.

I HEARD THE SOUND OF VOICES, SO I HID. A YOUNG GIRL RAN ALONG THE SIDE OF THE RIVER.

SUDDENLY HER FOOT SLIPPED AND SHE FELL INTO THE RIVER!

HE TORE THE GIRL FROM MY ARMS AND RAN BACK INTO THE WOOD. I FOLLOWED HIM. I DIDN'T REALLY KNOW WHY.

WHEN HE SAW ME, HE AIMED A GUN AT ME ...

AND FIRED!

BLAMM!

CRACK!

ARRGH!

I FELL TO THE GROUND AND THE MAN ESCAPED INTO THE WOOD.

I HAD SAVED SOMEONE'S LIFE, AND AS A REWARD I HAD RECEIVED A DREADFUL WOUND!

IN GREAT PAIN, I PROMISED THAT IN FUTURE I WOULD ONLY HATE PEOPLE AND INJURE THEM.

AFTER A FEW WEEKS, MY **WOUND** WAS BETTER, AND I CONTINUED MY JOURNEY. I DIDN'T FIND PLEASURE IN ANYTHING. I JUST FELT EXTREMELY UNHAPPY. AFTER TWO MONTHS, I ARRIVED NEAR GENEVA.

I HID MYSELF IN SOME FIELDS. I WAS TIRED AND HUNGRY. I FELL INTO A LIGHT SLEEP ...

... BUT A BEAUTIFUL CHILD WOKE ME UP.

HE RAN UP TO MY HIDING PLACE. I THOUGHT THAT HE WAS TOO YOUNG TO HATE ME.

AAAHHH!

IF I COULD TEACH HIM TO BE MY FRIEND, I WOULDN'T BE SO LONELY.

FRANKENSTEIN! YOU BELONG TO MY ENEMY!

YOU'LL BE MY FIRST VICTIM!

THE CHILD STILL *STRUGGLED* AND SHOUTED. I TOOK HOLD OF HIS *THROAT* TO MAKE HIM STOP ...

... AND IN A MOMENT, HE LAY DEAD AT MY FEET.

I TOO CAN CREATE *SORROW!* THIS DEATH WILL MAKE MY ENEMY *MISERABLE* AND DESTROY HIM!

I SAW SOMETHING THAT THE CHILD WAS WEARING. IT WAS A PICTURE OF A LOVELY WOMAN.

I REMEMBERED THAT SUCH BEAUTIFUL CREATURES WOULD NEVER BRING ME HAPPINESS.

I WENT TO FIND A HIDING PLACE AND ENTERED A *BARN*. A YOUNG WOMAN WAS SLEEPING THERE. SHE WAS LOVELY.

HERE IS ONE OF THOSE WHO WOULD NEVER SMILE AT ME.

WAKE UP, YOUR LOVER IS NEAR - SOMEONE WHO WOULD DIE TO HAVE ONE LOOK OF KINDNESS FROM YOU.

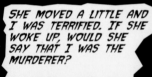

SHE MOVED A LITTLE AND I WAS TERRIFIED. IF SHE WOKE UP, WOULD SHE SAY THAT I WAS THE MURDERER?

I DECIDED THAT NOT I, BUT SHE, SHOULD SUFFER!

I MURDERED THE CHILD BECAUSE I WOULD NEVER HAVE THIS WOMAN'S KINDNESS, SO SHE SHOULD PAY FOR THE MURDER.

SHE MOVED AGAIN, AND I RAN AWAY.

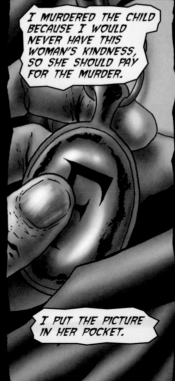

I PUT THE PICTURE IN HER POCKET.

FOR DAYS I STAYED NEAR THE PLACE WHERE I HAD MURDERED THE CHILD. THEN I CAME TO THESE MOUNTAINS. THERE IS SOMETHING I WISH FOR, AND ONLY YOU CAN GIVE IT TO ME.

YOU MUST PROMISE TO DO AS I ASK.

I AM ALONE AND MISERABLE.

PEOPLE HATE ME. YOU MUST CREATE A WOMAN WHO IS AS UGLY AS ME. SHE WILL NOT RUN AWAY FROM ME. YOU MUST CREATE THIS WOMAN.

VOLUME II
CHAPTER IX

ONLY YOU CAN DO THIS. YOU MUST NOT REFUSE.

NO!

SHALL I CREATE ANOTHER LIKE YOURSELF, WHO WILL HURT PEOPLE? I'LL NEVER AGREE TO IT!

I AM DANGEROUS BECAUSE I AM MISERABLE.

WHAT I AM ASKING FOR IS REASONABLE.

DO NOT REFUSE!

ALTHOUGH I FELT AFRAID, I SAW THE TRUTH OF WHAT HE SAID.

HOW CAN YOU LIVE IN WILD PLACES WITHOUT PEOPLE? YOU WANT PEOPLE'S LOVE AND YOU'LL RETURN TO FIND IT.

I PROMISE YOU THAT I WON'T.

WHY SHOULD I TRUST YOU?

IF YOU AGREE, NEITHER YOU, NOR ANYONE ELSE WILL EVER SEE US AGAIN. WE'LL SLEEP ON DRIED LEAVES AND EAT **NUTS** AND FRUIT.

WE'LL LIVE PEACEFULLY.

THEY WILL HATE YOU, AND THEN YOU'LL WANT TO KILL AGAIN.

THE LOVE OF ANOTHER WILL REMOVE THE CAUSE OF MY **CRIMES.**

I'LL DO IT, IF YOU AGREE TO LEAVE EUROPE FOREVER AND NEVER TO VISIT AN AREA WHERE PEOPLE LIVE.

I PROMISE THAT IF YOU GIVE ME THIS, YOU'LL NEVER SEE ME AGAIN!

GO HOME AND START YOUR WORK. I SHALL WATCH YOUR PROGRESS. WHEN YOU'RE READY, I'LL APPEAR!

HE WENT DOWN THE MOUNTAIN EXTREMELY QUICKLY AND DISAPPEARED.

WITH A HEAVY HEART, I WENT DOWN TOWARDS THE VALLEY.

I RETURNED TO MY FAMILY IN GENEVA. THEY WERE WORRIED BY MY WILD APPEARANCE. I SAID VERY LITTLE TO THEM, ALTHOUGH I LOVED THEM SO MUCH.

IF YOU FEEL THAT WAY, THEN WE WILL CERTAINLY BE HAPPY. TELL ME – WOULD YOU DISLIKE AN IMMEDIATE MARRIAGE?

FOR SOME TIME I COULD NOT REPLY TO MY FATHER.

THE IDEA OF AN IMMEDIATE MARRIAGE FILLED ME WITH **HORROR**.

I HADN'T DONE WHAT I HAD PROMISED THE **MONSTER**. I DIDN'T DARE TO BREAK MY PROMISE.

FIRST THE MONSTER HAD TO LEAVE WITH HIS **MATE**. THEN I COULD ENJOY THE HAPPINESS OF MARRIAGE IN PEACE.

I REMEMBERED THAT I NEEDED TO GO TO ENGLAND. I HAD TO GET NEW INFORMATION FOR MY TASK.

ALSO, I HAD TO BE AWAY FROM THOSE I LOVED WHILE I WORKED.

I **PERSUADED** MY FATHER TO AGREE TO THE TRIP.

HE HOPED IT WOULD BE GOOD FOR ME.

I COULD GO FOR A FEW MONTHS, OR EVEN A YEAR. HE ASKED CLERVAL TO GO WITH ME.

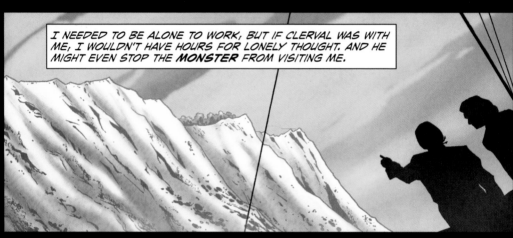

I NEEDED TO BE ALONE TO WORK, BUT IF CLERVAL WAS WITH ME, I WOULDN'T HAVE HOURS FOR LONELY THOUGHT. AND HE MIGHT EVEN STOP THE **MONSTER** FROM VISITING ME.

WE PLANNED THAT ELIZABETH AND I WOULD MARRY WHEN I RETURNED. FOR ME, THIS WAS MY **REWARD** FOR COMPLETING THE TASK I HATED.

I WAS AFRAID OF LEAVING MY FAMILY. MY **ENEMY** COULD ATTACK THEM WHILE I WAS AWAY.

BUT HE HAD PROMISED TO FOLLOW ME EVERYWHERE, SO WOULD HE NOT COME TO ENGLAND?

VOLUME III
CHAPTER II

WE DECIDED TO STAY IN LONDON FOR A FEW MONTHS.

IT WAS A WONDERFUL CITY BUT I COULDN'T ENJOY IT.

A DARK CLOUD HUNG OVER ME.

THIS IS LIVING!

CLERVAL WANTED TO MEET MEN WHO WERE CLEVER AND FULL OF NEW IDEAS. THIS WAS NOT IMPORTANT TO ME.

MY AIM WAS TO GET THE INFORMATION I NEEDED FOR MY TASK.

I TOOK MY LETTERS OF INTRODUCTION TO THE MOST FAMOUS NATURAL SCIENTISTS.

I ONLY VISITED THESE PEOPLE FOR THE INFORMATION THEY COULD GIVE ME.

I FELT *DESPAIR* WHEN I WAS WITH OTHER PEOPLE. I WASN'T LIKE THEM.

CLERVAL WAS HOW I HAD BEEN IN THE PAST. HE WANTED TO LEARN AND TO DO NEW THINGS. HE WAS ALSO WORKING TOWARDS ACHIEVING SOMETHING HE HAD WANTED FOR A LONG TIME.

HE WANTED TO GO TO INDIA SO THAT HE COULD BECOME A TRADER THERE.

HE WAS ALWAYS BUSY. I OFTEN REFUSED TO GO TO PLACES WITH HIM, SO THAT I COULD BE ALONE.

I BEGAN TO COLLECT THE MATERIALS THAT I NEEDED FOR MY NEW CREATION.

I HATED DOING IT.

AFTER A FEW MONTHS IN LONDON, WE RECEIVED AN INVITATION FROM A FRIEND IN THE NORTH OF SCOTLAND. I DIDN'T LIKE BEING WITH PEOPLE, BUT I WANTED VERY MUCH TO SEE MOUNTAINS AND **STREAMS** AGAIN. WE ACCEPTED THE INVITATION.

ON THE WAY TO EDINBURGH WE VISITED WINDSOR, OXFORD, MATLOCK AND THE CUMBERLAND LAKES.

I TOOK MY EQUIPMENT AND MATERIALS SO THAT I COULD FINISH MY WORK IN THE NORTH OF SCOTLAND.

HENRY LOVED THE BEAUTY OF EDINBURGH, BUT I WANTED TO FINISH THE JOURNEY.

SOMETIMES I THOUGHT THE **MONSTER** HAD FOLLOWED ME. I WAS AFRAID HE WOULD KILL HENRY BECAUSE I WASN'T WORKING FAST ENOUGH.

I WANTED TO FIND A PLACE THAT WAS VERY FAR FROM ANYWHERE ELSE. I CHOSE A SMALL, ROCKY ISLAND IN THE ORKNEYS. ONLY FIVE PEOPLE AND A FEW COWS LIVED THERE.

I LIVED IN A SMALL **HUT.** I WORKED DURING THE DAY, AND IN THE EVENING I WALKED ALONG THE STONY BEACH TO LISTEN TO THE **WAVES** AS THEY CRASHED AT MY FEET.

AS THE DAYS PASSED, I BEGAN TO HATE MY WORK MORE AND MORE. SOMETIMES I COULDN'T DO IT AT ALL ...

... AND AT OTHER TIMES, I WORKED DAY AND NIGHT. I BECAME RESTLESS AND NERVOUS. ALL THE TIME I WAS AFRAID OF MEETING THE **MONSTER**.

WHEN I WORKED ON MY FIRST EXPERIMENT, I FELT EXCITED. THIS TIME I FELT SICK.

VOLUME III
CHAPTER III

ONE EVENING I BEGAN TO THINK ABOUT WHAT I WAS DOING.

THREE YEARS EARLIER I HAD CREATED A MONSTER WHO HAD DONE **DREADFUL** THINGS.

NOW I WAS MAKING ANOTHER CREATURE. I DIDN'T KNOW WHAT SHE WOULD DO.

PERHAPS THEY WOULD HATE EACH OTHER. HE MIGHT THINK SHE WAS UGLY.

SHE MIGHT TURN AWAY FROM HIM. SHE MIGHT LEAVE HIM, AND MAKE HIM MORE **MISERABLE.**

OR THEY COULD HAVE CHILDREN WHO MIGHT BE DANGEROUS.

FOR THE FIRST TIME, I REALISED WHAT I HAD DONE. I HAD BOUGHT MY OWN PEACE AT THE PRICE, PERHAPS, OF THE EXISTENCE OF THE WHOLE **HUMAN RACE.**

SUDDENLY...

!?!

YES, HE HAD FOLLOWED ME. NOW HE HAD COME TO CLAIM WHAT I HAD PROMISED HIM.

HIS FACE WAS FULL OF EVIL.

I FELT MAD WHEN I THOUGHT OF MY PROMISE TO CREATE ANOTHER MONSTER LIKE HIM.

THE MONSTER WATCHED IN **HORROR** AS I DESTROYED THE ONLY CREATURE THAT COULD BRING HIM HAPPINESS.

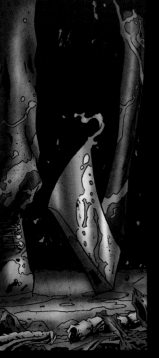

HE GAVE A CRY OF *DESPAIR* AND *REVENGE* AND DISAPPEARED.

I PROMISED MYSELF THAT I WOULD NEVER WORK ON THIS TASK AGAIN.

SEVERAL HOURS PASSED. THEN I HEARD THE SOUND OF A BOAT. SOMEBODY LANDED NEAR MY HOUSE.

YOU HAVE DESTROYED YOUR WORK! DO YOU INTEND TO BREAK YOUR PROMISE TO ME? DO YOU DARE TO DESTROY MY HOPES?

YES, I WILL BREAK MY PROMISE. I WILL NEVER CREATE ANOTHER LIKE YOU AGAIN!

REMEMBER THAT I HAVE POWER.

YOU ARE MY CREATOR, BUT I AM YOUR *MASTER*. OBEY!

BEFORE YOU KILL ME, BE SURE OF YOUR OWN SAFETY!

HE DISAPPEARED IN HIS BOAT, AND ALL WAS SILENT AGAIN.

I THOUGHT AGAIN OF HIS WORDS ...

'I SHALL BE WITH YOU ON YOUR **WEDDING** NIGHT'.

THAT WAS GOING TO BE THE DAY OF MY DEATH. I DID NOT FEEL AFRAID. I FELT SORRY FOR ELIZABETH. I DECIDED NOT TO DIE WITHOUT A FIGHT.

THE NEXT DAY, I RECEIVED A LETTER FROM CLERVAL. HE ASKED ME TO JOIN HIM AGAIN. THE LETTER BROUGHT ME BACK TO REAL LIFE AND I DECIDED TO LEAVE THE ISLAND.

I PACKED UP MY EQUIPMENT AND THE PARTS OF THE UNFINISHED CREATURE. VERY EARLY THE NEXT MORNING, I SAILED OUT AND THREW THEM INTO THE SEA.

THE AIR WAS SO PURE THAT I DECIDED TO STAY LONGER ON THE WATER. EVENTUALLY CLOUDS HID THE MOON, EVERYTHING WAS DARK AND I HEARD ONLY THE SOUND OF THE BOAT. IN A SHORT TIME, I FELL ASLEEP.

WHEN I WOKE UP, THE SUN WAS QUITE HIGH IN THE SKY. THE WIND WAS HIGH TOO, AND THE **WAVES** WERE THREATENING THE SAFETY OF MY BOAT.

THE WIND HAD DRIVEN ME A LONG WAY FROM THE COAST.

WHEN I TRIED TO CHANGE DIRECTION, WATER QUICKLY FILLED THE BOAT. I COULD ONLY SAIL WITH THE WIND BEHIND ME.

I LOOKED AT THE SEA. IT WAS GOING TO BE MY **GRAVE.**

MONSTER! YOU'VE GOT WHAT YOU WANTED!

SOME HOURS PASSED IN THIS WAY ...

... BUT SLOWLY THE WIND BECAME GENTLER AND THE SEA BECAME CALMER. I WAS FEELING SICK AND VERY TIRED WHEN SUDDENLY I SAW LAND.

I CRIED WITH JOY. I KNEW I WAS FINALLY SAFE.

101

I WAS TAKEN TO THE JUDGE, AN OLD MAN WITH CALM AND KIND MANNERS. HE LOOKED AT ME, HOWEVER, QUITE UNKINDLY.

WHO IS APPEARING AS A **WITNESS**?

I AM, SIR.

I HAD BEEN OUT IN MY BOAT WITH MY **BROTHER-IN-LAW** DANIEL NUGENT.

AS I WAS WALKING HOME ALONG THE BEACH, I HIT MY FOOT ON THE BODY OF A MAN. HIS CLOTHES WERE DRY. SOMEONE HAD KILLED HIM.

THERE WERE BLACK **FINGERMARKS** ON HIS NECK.

I REMEMBERED MY BROTHER'S MURDER, AND I FELT EXTREMELY SHAKEN.

MR. KIRWIN SAW THAT I WAS BADLY AFFECTED. OF COURSE HE THOUGHT I WAS **GUILTY**.

MY NAME IS DANIEL NUGENT, SIR.

JUST BEFORE WE FOUND THE BODY, I SAW A MAN IN A BOAT, QUITE CLOSE TO THE **SHORE**.

IT LOOKED LIKE THE SAME BOAT THAT THIS MAN HAS JUST LANDED IN.

A WOMAN ALSO SAW A MAN IN A BOAT. HE SAILED AWAY FROM THE PLACE WHERE THE BODY WAS FOUND.

THEY ALL AGREED THAT THE STRONG WIND HAD DRIVEN ME BACK TO THE **SHORE** – TO WHERE I HAD LEFT THE BODY.

SHOW HIM THE BODY.

I WANT TO SEE HOW HE REACTS.

I WAS CALM.

I KNEW THAT THE PEOPLE ON THE ISLAND I HAD LEFT COULD **PROVE** MY **INNOCENCE**. I WAS TALKING TO THEM WHEN THE BODY WAS FOUND.

NO!! MY DEAREST HENRY!! NOT YOU TOO!!!

I HAVE ALREADY DESTROYED TWO PEOPLE ...

... BUT YOU, CLERVAL, MY FRIEND ...

THE SIGHT OF HENRY WAS TOO MUCH FOR ME. I FELL DOWN IN A **FIT**.

103

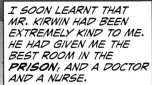

I SOON LEARNT THAT MR. KIRWIN HAD BEEN EXTREMELY KIND TO ME. HE HAD GIVEN ME THE BEST ROOM IN THE **PRISON**, AND A DOCTOR AND A NURSE.

ONE DAY, WHILE I WAS SLOWLY **RECOVERING**, HE VISITED ME.

105

... AND SOMEONE HAS COME TO VISIT YOU.

FATHER! YOU'RE SAFE!

AND ELIZABETH?

AND ERNEST?

ALL ARE SAFE.

WHAT A PLACE THIS IS, MY SON!

YOU TRAVELLED TO FIND HAPPINESS, BUT SOMETHING TERRIBLE SEEMS TO FOLLOW YOU.

AND POOR CLERVAL!

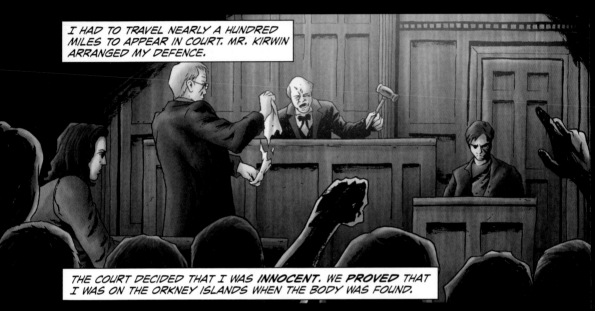

I HAD TO TRAVEL NEARLY A HUNDRED MILES TO APPEAR IN COURT. MR. KIRWIN ARRANGED MY DEFENCE.

THE COURT DECIDED THAT I WAS **INNOCENT**. WE **PROVED** THAT I WAS ON THE ORKNEY ISLANDS WHEN THE BODY WAS FOUND.

I WAS ALLOWED TO GO FREE. I COULD BREATHE FRESH AIR, AND GO HOME. BUT FOR ME, EVERYWHERE WAS HATEFUL. I OFTEN WANTED TO END MY LIFE, BUT I STILL HAD ONE DUTY. I HAD TO LOOK AFTER THE PEOPLE I LOVED. AND I HAD TO FIGHT THE MURDERER.

VOLUME III
CHAPTER V

WHEN WE REACHED PARIS, I RECEIVED A LETTER FROM ELIZABETH.

... TELL ME, DEAREST VICTOR - DO YOU LOVE ANOTHER?

I LOVE YOU, BUT IT IS YOUR HAPPINESS THAT I DESIRE.

- ELIZABETH

I REMEMBERED THE **MONSTER'S** THREAT: 'I SHALL BE WITH YOU ON YOUR **WEDDING** NIGHT!'

HE HAD DECIDED TO KILL ME ON THAT NIGHT. SWEET ELIZABETH! I WOULD DIE TO MAKE HER HAPPY.

MY DEAREST ELIZABETH, I AM AFRAID THAT LITTLE HAPPINESS REMAINS FOR US ON EARTH. HOWEVER, ALL MY FUTURE HAPPINESS IS CENTRED ON YOU. I PROMISE MYSELF TO YOU AND NO ONE ELSE.

I HAVE ONE, **DREADFUL** SECRET WHICH WILL FILL YOU WITH **HORROR.** I WILL TELL IT TO YOU THE DAY AFTER OUR MARRIAGE. UNTIL THEN, DO NOT MENTION IT.

- VICTOR

WE RETURNED TO GENEVA. ELIZABETH WELCOMED ME WARMLY.

ELIZABETH HAD **INHERITED** FROM HER FAMILY A SMALL HOUSE BY LAKE COMO. WE PLANNED TO SPEND OUR FIRST DAYS THERE. AFTER THE **WEDDING**, WE WENT BY BOAT TO EVIAN.

YOU'RE SAD, MY LOVE.

LET ME ENJOY THE HAPPINESS OF TODAY, AFTER ALL I HAVE SUFFERED.

BE HAPPY, MY DEAR VICTOR.

SOMETHING WHISPERS TO ME THAT I MUSTN'T **LOOK FORWARD TO** HAPPINESS, BUT I WON'T LISTEN TO SUCH A VOICE.

WHAT A BEAUTIFUL DAY! HO[W] HAPPY AND CALM NATURE LOOKS.

THOSE WERE THE LAST MOMENTS OF MY LIFE WHEN I FELT HAPPY.

AS WE REACHED THE **SHORE**, MY FEAR RETURNED. IT HAS STAYED WITH ME AND WILL STAY FOREVER.

WE TOOK A SHORT WALK ALONG THE **SHORE** AND ADMIRED THE LOVELY SCENE.

SUDDENLY THE WIND GREW STRONGER AND A HEAVY STORM OF RAIN CAME DOWN. I WAS ANXIOUS, AND HELD TIGHTLY TO MY **GUN**.

WHAT ARE YOU AFRAID OF, VICTOR?

OH! IT'S JUST THE STORM.

IT'S A **DREADFUL** NIGHT.

PLEASE GO TO BED, MY LOVE. I'LL JOIN YOU LATER.

VICTOR ...

SHE LEFT ME, AND I SEARCHED THE HOUSE FOR THE MONSTER ...

... BUT I FOUND NOTHING.

AAAAHH!!!

SHRIEK!!

AS I HEARD THE SCREAM, I REALISED WHAT WAS HAPPENING!

ELIZABETH!!!

I FAINTED.

BANG!

HE RAN AWAY AND INTO THE LAKE.

THE SOUND OF THE **GUN** ATTRACTED A CROWD, WHO HELPED ME LOOK FOR THE **MONSTER.** AFTER SEVERAL HOURS WE RETURNED. WE HADN'T FOUND HIM. MANY OF THE PEOPLE THOUGHT THAT I HAD IMAGINED HIM.

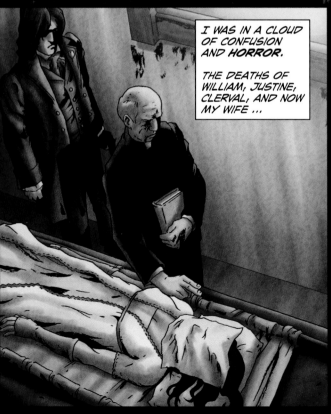

I WAS IN A CLOUD OF CONFUSION AND **HORROR.**

THE DEATHS OF WILLIAM, JUSTINE, CLERVAL, AND NOW MY WIFE ...

... MY FATHER AND ERNEST MIGHT DIE NEXT!

I DECIDED TO RETURN TO GENEVA AS QUICKLY AS POSSIBLE.

MY FATHER AND ERNEST WERE ALIVE, BUT MY FATHER WAS VERY BADLY AFFECTED BY ELIZABETH'S DEATH.

IT WAS TOO MUCH FOR HIM, AND A FEW DAYS LATER HE DIED IN MY ARMS.

WHAT HAPPENED TO ME THEN? ... I DON'T KNOW. I LOST **CONSCIOUSNESS.** WHEN I WOKE UP, I WAS ALONE IN A DARK ROOM IN A **PRISON.** I HAD BEEN THERE FOR MANY MONTHS.

WHEN I WAS ALLOWED TO LEAVE, I VISITED A JUDGE IN THE TOWN. I WANTED TO TELL HIM ABOUT THE **MONSTER**.

SIR, I KNOW WHO MURDERED MY BROTHER AND WIFE.

I WANT YOU TO HELP ME TO FIND HIM.

I'LL DO ALL THAT I CAN, SIR.

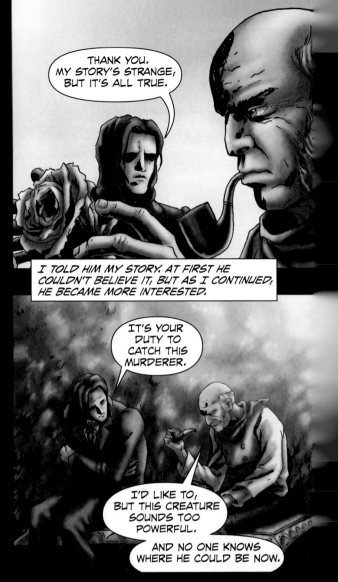

THANK YOU. MY STORY'S STRANGE, BUT IT'S ALL TRUE.

I TOLD HIM MY STORY. AT FIRST HE COULDN'T BELIEVE IT, BUT AS I CONTINUED, HE BECAME MORE INTERESTED.

IT'S YOUR DUTY TO CATCH THIS MURDERER.

I'D LIKE TO, BUT THIS CREATURE SOUNDS TOO POWERFUL.

AND NO ONE KNOWS WHERE HE COULD BE NOW.

YOU REFUSE TO HELP ME!

THEN I'LL FIND HIM MYSELF! I'LL DESTROY HIM!

I LEFT HIS HOUSE ANGRILY. I WENT AWAY TO THINK ABOUT WHAT TO DO.

VOLUME III
CHAPTER VII

REVENGE GAVE ME STRENGTH.
I DECIDED TO LEAVE GENEVA FOREVER.

BUT FIRST I FOUND MYSELF BY THE **GRAVES** OF WILLIAM, ELIZABETH AND MY FATHER.

THEIR **SPIRITS** SEEMED TO FLY AROUND. I FELT VERY ANGRY.

I WILL FOLLOW THE **MONSTER** WHO HAS CAUSED THESE DEATHS UNTIL EITHER HE DIES OR I DIE!

LET HIM FEEL THE **DREADFUL** SADNESS THAT I FEEL!

HA HA HA HA HA! I'M HAPPY.

YOU'VE DECIDED TO LIVE, MISERABLE CREATURE!

I RAN TOWARDS HIM, BUT HE ESCAPED.

I RAN AFTER HIM, AND HAVE BEEN FOLLOWING HIM FOR MANY MONTHS.

I FOLLOWED HIM THROUGH FRANCE AND THEN TO THE BLACK SEA. THEN I WENT AFTER HIM THROUGH RUSSIA.

HE LEFT MESSAGES ON TREES OR STONES TO GUIDE ME. I BOUGHT A **SLEDGE** AND DOGS. I **CROSSED** THE SNOWS QUICKLY AND CAME CLOSER TO HIM.

WHEN I HAD ALMOST REACHED HIM, THE ICE BROKE. THE SEA CAME BETWEEN US AND I WAS LEFT ON A PIECE OF ICE.

WHEN I SAW YOUR SHIP, I MANAGED TO MOVE TOWARDS IT.

YOU SAVED ME WHEN I WAS CLOSE TO DEATH. I STILL FEAR DEATH BECAUSE I HAVEN'T COMPLETED MY TASK. IF I DIE, WALTON, FIND HIM AND KILL HIM. PROMISE ME, PLEASE.

LETTER - SEPTEMBER 7TH, 17--

THE MATTER IS SETTLED. I HAVE AGREED TO RETURN IF WE GET FREE OF THE ICE. I AM VERY DISAPPOINTED.

September 12th, 17--

It is over. I am returning to England. I have lost my hopes of glory - and I have lost my friend.

Three days ago, the ice began to move. Islands of ice broke off in all directions. We were in great danger, but we could do nothing. My unfortunate guest was so ill that he had to stay in bed.

HURRAH!

YEAH!

HOORAY!

THEY'RE HAPPY BECAUSE THIS MEANS WE'LL SOON GO BACK TO ENGLAND.

ARE YOU REALLY GOING TO GO BACK?

YES. I CAN'T LEAD THEM INTO GREATER DANGER.

I WON'T COME WITH YOU. I MUST DO WHAT I HAVE PROMISED.

I'M WEAK, BUT THE **SPIRITS** WHO HELP ME WILL GIVE ME STRENGTH.

HE TRIED TO GET OUT OF HIS BED, BUT IT WAS TOO MUCH FOR HIM. HE FELL BACK AND **FAINTED**.

THE DOCTOR TOLD ME THAT HE WOULD ONLY LIVE FOR A FEW HOURS.

Ah! My strength has gone. I will soon die, and my **enemy** may still be alive.

I was mad when I made him. He destroyed my family and friends. He ought to die so that he doesn't kill anyone else.

But I can't ask you to leave your country and friends to find him.

I DON'T WANT YOU TO FEEL SORRY FOR ME. I'M CONTENT TO SUFFER ALONE.

AT ONE TIME I HOPED FOR HUMAN LOVE, BUT MY **CRIMES** HAVE PLACED ME BELOW THE LOWEST ANIMAL.

WHEN I REMEMBER ALL THAT I HAVE DONE, I CANNOT BELIEVE THAT I AM THE SAME CREATURE THAT AT ONE TIME WANTED ONLY BEAUTY AND GOODNESS.

BUT IT IS SO: THE FALLEN **ANGEL** BECOMES A **DEVIL.**

SOON I WILL DIE AND MY UNHAPPINESS WILL BE OVER. I WILL BE HAPPY AT LAST IN THE PAIN OF THE FIRE!
AAARRRRGGGHHH!!!
MY SPIRIT WILL SLEEP IN PEACE.

Frankenstein

End

Glossary

A

adopt /əˈdɒpt/ – (adopts, adopting, adopted) If you adopt someone else's child, you take it into your own family and make it legally your own.

Alpine /ˈælpaɪn/ Something that is Alpine is of or relating to high mountains or to the Alps mountain range in Europe.

angel /ˈeɪndʒəl/ – (angels) Angels are spiritual beings that some people believe are God's messengers and servants in heaven.

arrest /əˈrest/ – (arrests, arresting, arrested) When the police arrest someone, they take them to a police station in order to decide whether they should be charged with an offence. *Police arrested five young men in connection with the attacks.*

astonishing /əˈstɒnɪʃɪŋ/ Something that is astonishing is very surprising.

B

barn /baːn/ – (barns) A barn is a building on a farm in which crops or animal food are kept.

bear /beə/ If you bear something difficult, you accept it and are able to deal with it. *They have to bear living in constant fear. / He can't bear to talk about it.*

beat /biːt/ – (beats, beating, beat, beaten) When your heart or pulse beats, it continually makes regular rhythmic movements. *My heart beat faster.*

blame /bleɪm/ – (blames, blaming, blamed) If you blame a person or thing for something bad, or if you think or say they are to blame, you think or say that they are responsible for it. *He resigned, blaming himself for the team's defeat. / Miller could have blamed others, but he took responsibility.*

board /bɔːd/ – (boards, boarding, boarded) When you go on board a train, ship, or aircraft, you get on it.

brave /breɪv/ Someone who is brave is willing to do dangerous things, and does not show fear in difficult or dangerous situations. *She became an extremely brave horsewoman. / Are you brave enough to face up to this challenge?*

brother-in-law /ˈbrʌðə ɪn lɔː/ – (brothers-in-law) Someone's brother-in-law is the brother of their husband or wife, or the man who is married to their sister.

C

captain /ˈkæptɪn/ – (captains) A captain is a military officer or middle rank. *A captain in the army.* The captain of an aeroplane or ship is the officer in charge of it.

Christian /ˈkrɪstʃən/ – (Christians) A Christian or a Christian person follows the teachings of Jesus Christ.

confess /kənˈfes/ – (confesses, confessing, confessed) If you confess to doing something wrong or something that you are ashamed of, you admit that you did it. *He confessed to seventeen murders. / Ed confessed that he was worried.*

cottage /ˈkɒtɪdʒ/ – (cottages) A cottage is a small house, usually in the country.

courtyard /ˈkɔːtjɑːd/ – (courtyards) A courtyard is a flat open area of ground surrounded by buildings or walls.

crime /kraɪm/ – (crimes) A crime is an illegal action or activity for which a person can be punished by law. *It's not a crime to be stupid.*

cross /krɒs/ – (crosses, crossing, crossed) If you cross a room, road, or area of land, you move to the other side of it. If you cross to a place, you move over a room, road, or area in order to reach that place.

curse /kɜːs/ – (curses, cursing, cursed) If you curse someone or something, you say insulting things to them or complain strongly about them because you are angry with them. *We started driving again, cursing the delay. / He cursed himself for not making a note of his address.*

D

decay /dɪˈkeɪ/ – (decays, decaying, decayed) When something decays, it becomes rotten. This process is called decay. *The smell of decaying bodies sits in the air.*

deserve /dɪˈzɜːv/ – (deserves, deserving, deserved) If you say that someone deserves something, you mean that they should have or do it because of their qualities and actions. *'He deserved to suffer,' said Paul angrily. / Every patient deserves better care.*

despair /dɪˈspeə/ If you feel despair, you feel that everything is wrong and that nothing will improve. *I looked at my wife in despair.*

destiny /ˈdestɪni/ – (destinies) A person's destiny is everything that happens to them during their life, including what will happen in the future. Destiny is the force which some people believe controls the things that happen to you. *It is destiny that brings people together.*

devil /ˈdevəl/ – (devils) A devil is an evil spirit.

disease /dɪˈziːz/ – (diseases) A disease is an illness which affects people, animals, or plants. *... the spread of disease in the area. / ... heart disease*

disgusting /dɪsˈɡʌstɪŋ/ If you say that something is disgusting, you think it is extremely unpleasant or unacceptable. *... one of the most disgusting sights I ever* saw. / *I think it's disgusting that people over 65 have to pay tax.*

dreadful /ˈdredfʊl/ If you say that something is dreadful, you mean that it is very unpleasant or very poor in quality. *They told us the dreadful news. / My financial situation is dreadful.*

dull /dʌl/ – (duller, dullest) A dull colour or light is not bright. *The stamp was a dark, dull blue colour.*

Œ E

embrace /ɪmˈbreɪs/ – (embraces, embracing, embraced) When you embrace someone, you put your arms around them in order to show your affection for them. This action is called an embrace. *The couple embraced each other. / John and Anne were locked in an embrace.*

enemy /ˈenəmi/ – (enemies) Your enemy is someone who intends to harm you. In a war, the enemy is the army or country that you are fighting. 'Enemy' can take the singular or plural form of the verb for this meaning. *The enemy attacked the city from all sides. / The enemy are all around us.*

European /yʊərəˈpiən/ – A person who comes from Europe.

evil /ˈiːvəl/ – (evils) Evil is used to refer to all the wicked and bad things that happen in the world. *... the battle between good and evil.* An evil is a very unpleasant or harmful situation or activity. *... the evils of racism.* If you describe someone or something as evil, you mean that they are wicked and cause harm to people. *This was a cowardly and evil act.*

F F

faint /feɪnt/ – (faints, fainting, fainted) If you faint, or if you fall into a faint, you lose consciousness for a short time.

fingermark /ˈfɪŋɡəmaːk/ – (fingermarks) A fingermark is a mark made by a finger.

fit /fɪt/ – (fits) If someone has a fit, they suddenly lose consciousness and their body makes uncontrollable movements.

flash /flæʃ/ – (flashes) A flash of light is a sudden, short burst of it. *... a sudden flash of lightning*

forgive /fəˈɡɪv/ – (forgives, forgiving, forgave, forgiven) If you forgive someone who has done something wrong, you stop being angry with them. *She forgave him for stealing her money.*

frozen /ˈfrəʊzən/ If the ground is frozen, it has become very hard because the weather is very cold. *It was bitterly cold and the ground was frozen.* If you say that you are frozen, you mean that you are very cold. *He touched his frozen face.*

funeral /ˈfjuːnərəl/ – (funerals) A funeral is a ceremony for the burial or cremation of someone who has died. *His funeral will be on Thursday at Blackburn Cathedral.*

G G

glory /ˈɡlɔːri/ – (glories) Glory is fame and admiration that you get for an achievement. *It was her moment of glory.*

grave /ɡreɪv/ – (graves) A grave is a place where a dead person is buried.

graveyard /ˈɡreɪvjaːd/ – (graveyards) A graveyard is an area of land where dead people are buried.

great /ɡreɪt/ – (greater, greatest) 'Great' is used to emphasise the large amount or degree of something. *She had great difficulty in keeping her eyes open.*

guilt /ɡɪlt/ Guilt is an unhappy feeling that you have because you have done something bad. *... his feeling of guilt towards his son.* Guilt is the fact that you have done something bad or illegal. *There was some evidence of Mr Brown's guilt.*

guilty /ˈɡɪlti/ – (guiltier, guiltiest) If someone is guilty of doing something bad or committing a crime, they have done a bad thing or committed a crime. *He was found guilty of causing death by dangerous driving. / If someone is guilty, he should be punished.*

gun /ɡʌn/ – (guns) A gun is a weapon from which bullets or pellets are fired.

H H

heaven /ˈhevən/ – (heavens) In some religions, heaven is said to be the place where God lives and where good people go when they die. *The stars shone brightly in the heavens.*

hell /hel/ – (hells) According to some religions, Hell is the place where the Devil lives, and where wicked people are sent to be punished when they die. If you say that a particular situation or place is hell, you are emphasising that it is extremely unpleasant.

horror /ˈhɒrə/ Horror is a strong feeling of alarm caused by something extremely unpleasant. *I felt numb with horror.*

human race /ˈhyuːmən reɪs/ You can refer to all the people in the world as the human race.

hut /hʌt/ – (huts) A hut is a small, simple building, often made of wood, mud, or grass.

I I

inherit /ɪnˈherɪt/ – (inherits, inheriting, inherited) If you inherit money or property, you receive it from someone who has died. *He inherited these paintings from his father.*

innocence /ˈɪnəsəns/ If someone proves their innocence, they prove that they are not guilty of a crime.

innocent /'ɪnəsənt/ If someone is innocent, they did not commit a crime which they have been accused of. *He was sure that the man was innocent of murder.*

L

lecture /'lektʃə/ – (lectures) A lecture is a talk that someone gives in order to teach people about a particular subject, usually at a university.

lightning /'laitnɪŋ/ Lightning is a bright flash of light in the sky that you see during a thunderstorm.

long /lɒŋ/ – (longs, longing, longed) If you long for something, you want it very much. *He longed for the winter to finish. / I'm longing to meet her.*

look forward to /lʊk 'fɔːwəd tuː/ When you look forward to something, you wait with pleasure for it to happen. *I look forward to going on holiday in summer.*

M

master /'maːstə/ – (masters) A servant's master is the man he or she works for. You use 'master' to describe someone's job when they are very skilled at it. *... a master chef*

mate /meɪt/ – (mates) An animal's mate is its sexual partner.

merchant /'mɜːtʃənt/ – (merchants) A merchant is a person whose business is buying or selling goods in large quantities. *... a carpet merchant*

miserable /'məzərəbəl/ If you are miserable, you are very unhappy.

Monsieur /məs'yɜr/ 'Monsieur' is the conventional French title of respect and term of address for a man, similar to 'Mister'.

monster /'mɒnstə/ – (monsters) A creature so ugly that it frightens people.

N

nobleman /'nəʊbəlmən/ – (noblemen) A nobleman is someone who belongs to a high social class or has a title.

nonsense /'nɒnsəns/ If you say that something spoken or written is nonsense, you mean that you consider it to be untrue or silly.

nut /nʌt/ – (nuts) The firmed shelled fruit of some trees and bushes are called nuts.

P

pale /peɪl/ – (paler, palest) If someone looks pale, their face is a lighter colour than usual, because they are ill, frightened, or shocked.

Paradise Lost – Poem written by the English poet John Milton in 1667 about the fall of Man that is, the expulsion of Adam and Eve from the Garden of Eden after falling into the temptation of Satan.

persuade /pə'sweɪd/ – (persuades, persuading, persuaded) If you persuade someone to do a particular thing, you get them to do it, usually by convincing them that it is a good idea. *My husband persuaded me to go to the concert.*

poet /'pəʊɪt/ – (poets) A poet is a person who writes poems.

prison /'prɪzən/ – (prisons) A prison is a building where criminals are kept.

professor /prə'fesə/ – (professors) A professor in a British university is the most senior teacher in a department. *In 1979, only 2% of British professors were female.* A professor in an American or Canadian university or college is a teacher there.

prove /pruːv/ – (proves, proving, proved, proven) If you prove that something is true, you show by means of argument or evidence that it is definitely true. *Professor Cantor has proven his theory. / This proves how much we love each other. / It has made me determined to prove him wrong.*

R

race /reɪs/ – (races) A race is one of the major groups which human beings can be divided into according to their physical features, such as their skin colour.

reasonable /'riːzənəbəl/ If you say that an expectation or explanation is reasonable, you mean that there are good reasons why it may be correct. *It seems reasonable to expect things to change.*

recover /rɪ'kʌvə/ – (recovers, recovering, recovered) When you recover from an illness or an injury, you become well again. *He is recovering from a knee injury.*

recovery /rɪ'kʌvəri/ – (recoveries) If a sick person makes a recovery, he or she becomes well again. *He made a complete recovery.*

repay /rɪ'peɪ/ – (repays, repaying, repaid) If you repay a debt, you pay back the money you owe to somebody. If you repay a favour that someone did for you, you do something or give them something in return. *It was very kind. I don't know how I can repay you.*

revenge /rɪ'vendʒ/ Revenge involves hurting someone who has hurt you. *The other children took revenge on the boy, claiming he was a school bully. / They said that the attack was in revenge for the killing of their leader.*

reward /rɪ'wɔːd/ – (rewards) A reward is something that you are given because you have behaved well, worked hard, or provided a service to the community. *As a reward for good behaviour, give your child a new toy.*

S

scream /skriːm/ – (screams, screaming, screamed) When someone screams, they make a loud high-pitched cry, called a scream, usually because they are in pain or frightened. *He staggered around the room, screaming in agony.* If you scream something, you shout it in a loud high-pitched voice. *He grabbed Anthea and screamed abuse at her.*

sentence /ˈsentəns/ – (sentences, sentencing, sentenced) When judges sentence someone, they state in court what the person's punishment will be. *The court sentenced him to five years' imprisonment.*

servant /ˈsɜːvənt/ – (servants) A servant is someone who is employed to work in another person's house, for example, to cook or clean.

shade /ʃeɪd/ Shade is a cool area of darkness where the sun does not reach. *These plants need some shade, humidity and fresh air.*

shelter /ˈʃeltə/ – (shelters) A shelter is a small building or covered place which is made to protect people from bad weather or danger. If a place provides shelter, it provides protection from bad weather or danger. *The number of families seeking shelter rose by 17%.*

shore /ʃɔː/ – (shores) The shore of a sea, lake, or wide river is the land along the edge of it.

sledge /sledʒ/ – (sledges) A sledge is a vehicle for travelling over snow. It consists of a frame which slides on two strips of wood or metal.

sorrow /ˈsɒrəʊ/ – (sorrows) Sorrow is a feeling of deep sadness or regret. *It was a time of great sorrow.* Sorrows are events or situations that cause deep sadness. *... the joys and sorrows of everyday living.*

spirit /ˈspɪrɪt/ – (spirits) A person's spirit is a part of them that is not physical and that is believed to remain alive after their death. A spirit is a ghost or supernatural being.

stream /striːm/ – (streams) A stream is a small narrow river. A stream of things is a large number of them occurring one after another. *... a never-ending stream of jokes. / We had a constant stream of visitors.* If a mass of people, liquid or light, streams somewhere, it enters or moves there in large amounts. *Tears streamed down their faces.*

struggle /ˈstrʌɡəl/ – (struggles, struggling, struggled) If you struggle when you are being held, you twist and turn your body in order to try to get free. *I struggled to get free, but he was a strong man.*

stupidly /ˈstjuːpɪdlɪ/ If you say someone is doing something stupidly, you mean they are showing a lack of good judgement or intelligence and they are not at all sensible in what they are doing. *We had stupidly been looking at the wrong figures.*

surround /səˈraʊnd/ – (surrounds, surrounding, surrounded) If something or someone is surrounded by something, that thing is situated all around them. ... *the fluid that surrounds the brain.*

throat /θrəʊt/ – (throats) Your throat is the back of your mouth and the top part of the tubes that go down into your stomach and your lungs. Your throat is the front part of your neck.

thunder /ˈθʌndə/ Thunder is the loud noise that you hear from the sky after a flash of lightning.

trial /ˈtraɪəl/ – (trials) A trial is the legal process in which a judge and jury listen to evidence and decide whether a person is guilty of a crime. *He was giving evidence at the trial of Gary Hart, aged 37.*

U

ugliness /ˈʌɡlɪnəs/ The ugliness of someone or something refers to its unattractive and unpleasant state. ... *the ugliness of the old and dirty town.*

V

victim /ˈvɪktɪm/ – (victims) A victim is someone who has been hurt or killed by someone or something. ... *the victims of violent crime.*

voyage /ˈvɔɪɪdʒ/ – (voyages) A voyage is a long journey on a ship or in a spacecraft.

W

wave /weɪv/ – (waves) A wave is a raised mass of water on the sea or a lake, caused by the wind or the tide.

wealth /welθ/ Wealth is a large amount of money or property owned by someone, or the possession of it. *His own wealth increased after he inherited some money from his uncle.*

wedding /ˈwedɪŋ/ – (weddings) A wedding is a marriage ceremony and the celebration that often takes place afterwards.

witness /ˈwɪtnəs/ – (witnesses, witnessing, witnessed) A witness to an event such as an accident or crime is a person who saw it. If you witness something, or if you are witness to it, you see it happen. *Anyone who witnessed the attack should call the police.* A witness is someone who appears in a court of law to say what they know about a crime or other event. *Eleven witnesses will be called to testify.*

wound /wuːnd/ – (wounds) A wound is an injury to your body, especially a cut or hole caused by a gun, knife, or similar weapon.

A Brief Biography of Mary Shelley

Mary Shelley was born Mary Wollstonecraft Godwin in London on 30th August, 1797. Both her parents were famous writers, philosophers and intellectuals of the late eighteenth century. Her mother, Mary Wollstonecraft, was the author of *A Vindication of the Rights of Woman*. This was an important early feminist work that encouraged women to think and act for themselves — as equals with men. William Godwin was similarly respected in England for his influential social and political ideas.

Wollstonecraft died ten days after giving birth to Mary, leaving her daughter in the care of her husband. William Godwin married his neighbour, Mary Jane Vial (Clairmont), when Mary was four years old. This marriage gave Mary and her older half-sister, Fanny, a mother, a stepbrother, Charles, and a stepsister, Claire (previously Jane). William and his new wife had a son in 1803.

National Portrait Gallery, London

Mary Wollstonecraft Godwin's remarkable background helped to determine her unusual character, because it allowed her to appreciate the most modern of ideas, as well as the chance to meet notable people such as the English poet Lord Byron. She didn't receive a formal education, but was taught to read and write at home. Her father encouraged her to be creative from an early age and she was allowed access to his extensive library. She was also allowed to listen to the political, philosophical, scientific and literary discussions of her father and his friends, such as the poets William Wordsworth and Samuel Taylor Coleridge.

Among these important literary figures that Mary was introduced to was Percy Bysshe Shelley, a famous young poet. Percy was nineteen years old, and had already been expelled from Oxford University. His relationship with his own family was troubled. Yet, Percy greatly admired William Godwin and began spending time in the Godwin home, along with his young wife Harriet Shelley and sister-in-law Eliza. Soon afterwards, Mary and Percy developed a relationship, despite the fact that Mary's father had forbidden them to meet.

When Mary was only sixteen years old, she and Percy ran

away together to tour France, Switzerland and Germany. The young lovers took Mary's stepsister, Claire, with them, but left Percy's pregnant wife Harriet, behind. Mary and Percy's affair soon became strained due to Harriet's demands, which worsened on their return to London. By now, Mary was also pregnant. However, in 1816, Harriet drowned herself in the Serpentine River in Hyde Park, London. To the outrage of society, Mary Wollstonecraft married Percy Shelley two weeks later, on 30th December 1816 at St Mildred's Church in London. Fortunately for the couple, Percy was heir to his grandfather's estate, which allowed them to free themselves from the financial strain they had previously experienced.

Mary and Percy's union was not only romantic but also literary. He edited her manuscript for *Frankenstein* (which Mary had begun while they were in Switzerland) and he also wrote the preface. *Frankenstein* was eventually completed in May 1817, but wasn't published until 1st January, 1818 when it became an instant bestseller. However, even then, Mary wasn't named as the author and many people incorrectly believed it to have been written by Percy Shelley. This was because the book was dedicated to William Godwin, whom everyone knew Percy greatly admired. In fact, *Frankenstein* wasn't published in Mary's name until 1831. Tragically for Mary, though, many terrible events occurred in the middle of the success of her novel. From 1815 to 1819, three of her four children died when they were babies. The Shelleys moved to Florence in October 1819, and in May 1822, they moved on to La Spezia. There, on 16th June, Mary and Percy's fifth child died before it was born. Barely a month later, Percy drowned off the shores of Tuscany. At the age of 25, Mary was already a widow and single mother.

Mary and her only surviving child, Percy Florence, left Italy in the summer of 1823 and returned to England. Always resourceful, Mary edited her husband's poetry and prose, publishing his *Posthumous Poems* in 1824 and his *Poetical Works and Letters* in 1839. Mary Shelley didn't remarry, but instead dedicated the rest of her time to her own writing. *Valperga* was published in 1823, *The Last Man* in 1826, *The Fortunes of Perkin Warbeck* in 1830, *Lodore* in 1835, and *Falkner* in 1837. However, none of these later works are as well known or as influential as her first novel, *Frankenstein*.

From 1839 onwards, serious illness plagued Mary. She lived to see her only child, Percy Florence, marry in 1848. Mary Wollstonecraft Shelley died on 1st February 1851 aged 53. The cause of death is recorded as 'Disease of the brain — supposed tumour in left hemisphere of long standing'. She is buried next to her parents at St. Peter's Church in Bournemouth.

Characters

Victor Frankenstein

The main character and narrator of most of the story. Victor begins his story as an innocent youth fascinated by scientific discovery, but finishes it as a broken man torn by grief and guilt. While studying at university, Frankenstein discovers the secret of life. He creates an intelligent but horrifying monster. However, he instantly regrets this creation, and tries to hide from his mistake. He keeps this monster a secret. Soon, it becomes obvious to all that he can't stop his monster from ruining his life and the lives of his loved ones.

Frankenstein's Monster

Formed from old body parts and strange chemicals, the monster is the extremely tall, very strong, and terrifyingly ugly creation of Victor Frankenstein. However, he has the mind of a newborn baby. Sensitive and smart, the monster tries to join human society, but every human he meets is afraid of him. At first he feels alone and abandoned. Soon, however, he feels angry and seeks revenge.

Elizabeth Lavenza

An orphan adopted by the Frankenstein family, and whom Victor eventually marries. She is of a similar age to Victor, and they are very close growing up. For most of the novel, Elizabeth waits patiently for Victor, while looking after his younger brothers, Ernest and William.

Robert Walton

The Arctic traveller. Walton's letters begin and end the story of *Frankenstein*. Walton rescues Victor Frankenstein from the ice and helps nurse him back to health. As he's recovering, Frankenstein tells Walton his story. Walton writes down the incredible tale in a series of letters addressed to his sister, Margaret Saville, in England.

Henry Clerval

Victor Frankenstein's cheerful childhood friend. Clerval helps Victor to recover his health after the creation of the monster. Clerval also begins to study science, and travels with Frankenstein.

Alphonse Frankenstein

Victor's father. Alphonse is very sympathetic toward his son and tries to teach him good values in life. He consoles Victor when he's in pain, and encourages him to remember the importance of family.

Caroline Frankenstein

Victor's mother. After her father dies, Caroline is looked after by, and later marries, Alphonse Frankenstein. She has three sons and adopts a daughter. She dies of scarlet fever, which she catches from Elizabeth, her adopted daughter, when Victor is seventeen.

Characters

William Frankenstein

Victor's youngest brother. The monster strangles William in the woods outside Geneva because he wants to hurt Victor. William's death saddens Victor. It burdens him with immense guilt about creating the monster.

Ernest Frankenstein

Victor's brother, born in Geneva, and looked after by Elizabeth after their mother dies.

Justine Moritz

A young girl who works for the Frankenstein household. Justine is blamed for William's murder. Although she is not guilty, Justine is executed anyway, which makes Victor feel even worse.

The De Laceys

A family of peasants. The father, Monsieur De Lacey, lives with his son and daughter, Felix and Agatha, and Felix's lover Safie. Frankenstein's monster teaches himself to speak by observing them. The monster desperately wants to be friends with the De Laceys. However, when he introduces himself to the family, they are scared of him and chase him away.

M. Waldman

A professor of chemistry. Waldman encourages Victor's interest in science. He sympathises with Victor's interest in a science that can explain the unexplainable, such as 'the origins of life'.

M. Krempe

A professor of natural science. Krempe dismisses Victor's study of the chemistry as a waste of time. He encourages Victor to begin new studies.

Mr. Kirwin

The magistrate who accuses Victor of Henry's murder.

Context of Frankenstein

Key Facts

Full title: *Frankenstein: or, The Modern Prometheus*
Author: Mary Wollstonecraft Shelley
Type of work: Novel
Genre (type of writing): Gothic science fiction
Language: English
Time and place written: Switzerland, 1816, and London, 1816–1817
Date of first publication: 1st January, 1818
Tense: Past
Tone: Romantic, emotional, fatalistic, Gothic
Setting: Geneva, France, the Swiss Alps, Ingolstadt, England, Scotland, Ireland, the northern ice in the 18th century.

'How I, then a young girl, came to think of and to dilate upon so very hideous an idea?'

In the summer of 1816, a well-educated young woman from England, Mary Wollstonecraft Godwin, travelled with her married lover, Percy Bysshe Shelley, to the Swiss Alps. Unusually for that time of year, rain kept them indoors. There, along with their friend the scientist and poet John William Polidori, they entertained themselves by reading old German ghost stories. The couple's neighbour and friend, well-known poet Lord Byron, soon began a competition to see who could write the best ghost story. Shelley wrote a story based on his life experiences, Byron wrote a bare fragment of a novel and Polidori is believed to have begun *The Vampyre*.

At first, Mary was lost for ideas, but she was nevertheless determined to write a story which would 'speak to the mysterious fears of our nature, and awaken thrilling horror – one to make the reader dread to look round, to curdle the blood, and quicken the beatings of the heart.' During one gathering of the group that summer, they debated the nature and origin of life. They discussed whether this origin would ever be discovered by modern science. Such conversations considerably affected Mary. It wasn't long afterwards that she imagined the birth of a human-made man, created almost as one would create an engine, and horrifying its creator. Mary's story had started; the monster had his creator.

By the end of the summer, it was Mary Wollstonecraft Godwin who took the prize in Byron's competition. She had created a terrifying story that was to become a bestseller in her own time, and a classic that still impacts on readers nearly two centuries later.

Plot
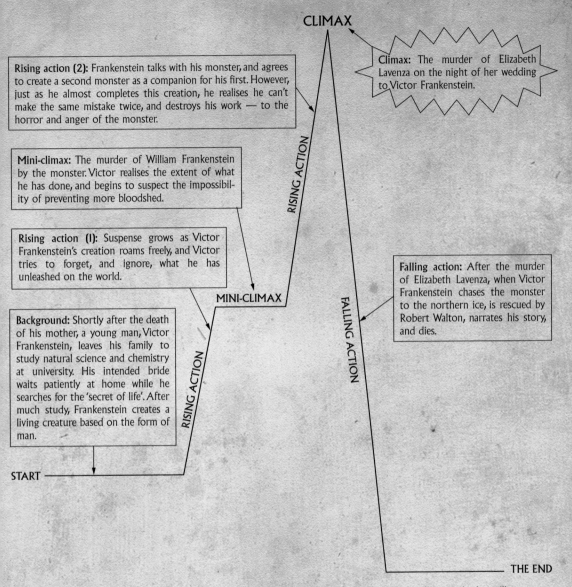

CLIMAX

Climax: The murder of Elizabeth Lavenza on the night of her wedding to Victor Frankenstein.

Rising action (2): Frankenstein talks with his monster, and agrees to create a second monster as a companion for his first. However, just as he almost completes this creation, he realises he can't make the same mistake twice, and destroys his work — to the horror and anger of the monster.

Mini-climax: The murder of William Frankenstein by the monster. Victor realises the extent of what he has done, and begins to suspect the impossibility of preventing more bloodshed.

Rising action (1): Suspense grows as Victor Frankenstein's creation roams freely, and Victor tries to forget, and ignore, what he has unleashed on the world.

Falling action: After the murder of Elizabeth Lavenza, when Victor Frankenstein chases the monster to the northern ice, is rescued by Robert Walton, narrates his story, and dies.

Background: Shortly after the death of his mother, a young man, Victor Frankenstein, leaves his family to study natural science and chemistry at university. His intended bride waits patiently at home while he searches for the 'secret of life'. After much study, Frankenstein creates a living creature based on the form of man.

RISING ACTION

RISING ACTION

MINI-CLIMAX

FALLING ACTION

START

THE END

Foreshadowing: Throughout his narrative, Victor uses words such as 'fate' and 'omen' to hint at the tragedy that will occur. Occasionally he pauses in his retelling as frightening memories come flooding back to him.

Primary narrator(s): Robert Walton, who, in his letters, quotes Victor Frankenstein's first-person narrative at length; Victor, in turn, quotes the monster's first-person narrative.

Secondary narrator(s): The lesser characters Elizabeth Lavenza and Alphonse Frankenstein also narrate parts of the story through their letters to Victor.

Point of view: The point of view shifts with the narration, from Robert Walton to Victor Frankenstein to Frankenstein's monster, then back to Walton. Occasionally Elizabeth and Alphonse's points of view are heard as well.

Hero and villain: Victor Frankenstein is both a classic mad scientist, crossing moral boundaries without concern, *and* a brave adventurer who travels into unknown scientific lands, not to be held responsible for the consequences of his explorations.

Themes: The danger and responsibility of knowledge; the wonder and beauty of Nature; the moral lesson that pride must have its fall; monstrosity* and secrecy.

Symbols: Fire, light

* If you describe something as monstrous you mean that it is very shocking or unfair.

Notes

Notes

Audio Track Listings

Frankenstein

OTHER CLASSICAL COMICS TITLES:

Henry V

Published

Macbeth

Published

Great Expectations

Forthcoming

Jane Eyre

Forthcoming